Trac oga

Into the Depth of Yoga

A guide to the essential practices
Of Himalayan School of Traditional Yoga

Traditional Yoga – Into the Depth of Yoga

First edition published by Gurulight 2020
Email: info@gurulight.com
Web: www.gurulight.com

ISBN: 978-81-935309-6-2

FOREWORD

Unit. Union. Unity.

Every creation is aligned by birth. Every being comes as a total unit by birth but usually leaves the earth, fragmented. Unlike other species, the fragmented state is even more pronounced in the human incarnation. Therefore, great ancient masters said, "It is easy to come and more difficult to go."

We are born as one unit and come with an agenda of experiencing many things from earth over time. As life takes its course, we leave behind fragments of mind over compelling memories or familiar desires and thus literally become slaves of existence. Yet, we call this compulsive, addictive binding – "life". When fears deliver tragedies in our life, we call it fate. When we entertain insecurities, when we become anxious about the future, when we compare, criticise, and suffer its implications, we become absent-minded or unconscious and thus lose the flavour as well as meaning of life. This is the average human existence in a modern world driven by technology that has made people self-centred islands.

What are our key faculties? Body. Mind. Intellect. Ego. Spirit. Body and spirit are units always. They stay aligned of their own accord. Body carries senses which are sensors for sensing life. Mind, intellect and ego process the data assimilated by the senses. Mind processes emotions. Intellect processes information. Ego processes matters connected to existence such as position, possessions and relations. Thus, various raw materials, inputs or data keep the processors on overdrive and fragmented. By nature, by default, no faculty is ever fragmented. The materials that it gets to handle keeps itbusy and fragmented. The pressure of various triggers from the world outside, responding and corresponding to the stored memories in the world inside, keep the waking state workload high.

The problem with an unconscious over-driven existence is the accumulation of unwanted fat in the system, the unprocessed data and the residual memory. They are the unseen residue, the inevitable backlog that produces the lack of contentment in everyday life. We can easily witness that in our everyday existence. The many dilemmas of life such as high-flying emotions, road rages, divorces from relations and activities, depression, complexes, comparisons, cravings, bindings, overemphasis on food, clothing, shelters, ornaments and so on. Time and again, repeatedly, we get inseparably engaged with life deeper and deeper. We forget that we are born free and have the right to remain free always. We can practically own nothing on earth and no one can own anybody. We can keep some things for some time until time takes us away from it all.

This is where we have to get back to basics urgently. Great masters have told us how to lead a healthy, meaningful and a refined existence beyond greed and gluttony. The art of being united. Body, mind, intellect, ego and spirit need to stay united as they are interconnected. They depend on each other for experiencing life on earth. So, aligning mind, intellect and ego with the body, uniting all faculties consciously, brings back our original state, that of a unit. When mind, intellect and ego roam around the world through the senses, they habitually crave for more. When mind, intellect and ego dive within, they roam over memories of experiences. This compels them to get back to the senses and try for more similar experiences outside, that the memories are made from. When we consciously restrain our mind inside, it learns to chew on the stored memories and digests them instead of procuring more and more of them unconsciously. Thus, the union of all faculties brings unity of being, leading to beingness.

Beingness is the state of a complete unit. The state of a unit is the state of perfection in alignment - body, mind, intellect, ego and spirit together as one unit. When consumption through senses stops, digestion becomes easy. System becomes clear. All the contaminated, putrefied memory fat is expelled from the system. More space gets generated inside. Less memories mean lesser thoughts, expressions and actions as well as no craving or compulsions. Peace. This also leads to zero ownership. Freedom. The state of perpetual freedom delivers the state of liberation. Liberation while living is indeed the state of not needing anything from the world outside, which also means absolute gratitude towards what has been provided as well as no fears. This state of no needs further matures into a state where, apart from the basic needs such as food, air, water and space, nothing else matters. It is living in detachment with full awareness that we own nothing on earth and we are grateful for what we have and the opportunity to be here, as whatever we are. Thus, Yoga is the science of staying liberated, through conscious connection with oneself, maintaining sensitivity, fluidity and flexibility. This science is fathomless, as deep and profound as subtleties of creation go. Yoga is unity. Yoga is staying united. Yoga is staying liberated.

BRAHMARISHI MOHANJI
Founder of Himalayan School of Traditional Yoga, Mohanji Foundation, ACT Foundation and other global initiatives such as Early Birds Club and World Consciousness Alliance
www.mohanji.org

Brahmarishi Mohanji

"I wish you tremendous awareness,
tremendous contentment
and deep connectivity to yourself."

Contents

ACKNOWLEDGEMENTS

The seeds of our own book on yoga were laid in the year 2016 when Mohanji set this as the next big priority to our dear Sanjay Sir (late Yogacharya Sanjay). While preliminary work started on it then, the book stayed in planning stages for quite a while with no concrete progress. Further, when Sanjay Sir died suddenly in a tragic road accident in May 2018, the book seemed to further recede in the list of priorities. It was only in late 2019 when we announced our next Teacher Training Course that the book gained momentum and it has finally taken shape in the form of the book that you are currently holding in your hand.

We are grateful to Usha Lakshminarayan for her tireless work on this book as the lead author for this book. Dr Rshikesan, a renowned expert in yoga, offered his advice and comments on fine tuning the contents of this book. We are also grateful to Devi Mohan for her inputs, encouragement and support in bringing this book to life. Thank you to Pooja Gandhi and Preethi Gopalarathnam for their inputs to the book, as well as to Nikolina Dragojevic for her assistance with the book. We are grateful to Dr K Unnikrishnan and Dr Revathy TI of Himalayan School of Traditional Languages, and to Kishore Mundanat for their assistance with the Sanskrit diacritic text. Photo credits go to Shanthi Mohan who worked on the photographs that are featured in this book, with the able assistance of Kiran Magare in processing the pictures. We are thankful to Gonika Yogini and Rohit Chohan for being perfect yoga models demonstrating all the techniques featured in the book. We are also thankful to Mr Narinder Rohmetra and Mr Suman Gupta for being gracious hosts for the photo shoot for this book.

Our thanks to Zoran Stefanovski (Mohana Hanumatananda) for designing our beautiful book cover. Our sincere thanks also to Mirko Trbusic and Gargi Sankpal for their creative inputs on the book layout. We are thankful to Mr Venkatraman for his work on the layout and typesetting, and Mr Sarathy Raghavan and his team at Usha Multigraphs.

The book would not be complete without acknowledging Sanjay Sir who laid the foundation for this school, and whose loving guidance is felt even today when he's no longer in the physical body. Lastly, we offer this book as flowers to the feet of our guru, Brahmarishi Mohanji, whose inspiration and constant guidance provide the very life force for the institution.

Madhusudan Rajagopalan
Director, Himalayan School of Traditional Yoga

GENERAL GUIDELINES FOR ĀSANA AND PRĀNĀYĀMA

1. The place for doing yoga practice should be clean, insect free, ventilated and well lighted.
2. The practice is to be done on empty stomach, ideally in the morning or 3 to 4 hours after meals and about 45 minutes after light beverages.
3. One should not have food immediately after yoga practice, but food can be taken 30 minutes after yoga practice.
4. If possible, yoga practice is desirable after a bath. Otherwise a bath can be taken after half an hour of yoga practice.
5. Dress for yoga practice should be light, clean and not too tight, as suited to weather conditions. Dress should not obstruct body movements.
6. The mat for yoga practice should be clean, not too hard or too soft or slippery.
7. Proper natural, nutritious, balanced food in moderation is to be consumed.
8. If physical exercises are done, then keep a gap of half an hour between yoga practice and physical exercises.
9. Yoga practice can be done any time of the day but it is more beneficial if done in the morning and at a fixed time of the day.
10. Sequencing and selection of yoga practices shall be as per the capacity of the practitioner.
11. The expenditure of energy should be minimum, and practices are to be ideally effortless.
12. The internal awareness towards breathing, joint movements and stretching of muscles is to be maintained at all times while doing the practice.
13. Āsana practice should be slow and continuous. Jerky haphazard movements are to be avoided, and one should practice as per one's capacity only. Excessive force or effort should not be applied.
14. Contra indications of the practice are to be considered before starting the practice.
15. Breathing is through the nose only unless specific instructions are given for certain practices
16. Yoga can be practiced by all age groups, male and female.
17. There should not be any pain in any part of body while doing the practice and one should stop the practice if discomfort persists and consult a physician or senior yoga teacher.
18. Āsana practice should start with right side movements to maintain uniformity. In final position of the posture, bring awareness to slow, smooth breathing.
19. All standing postures should be done with eyes open. Others can be done with closed eyes to bring awareness and to go inwards, but it is optional.

I Light Yogic Exercises

I-1 Pādāṅgulī Naman (Toe Bending)

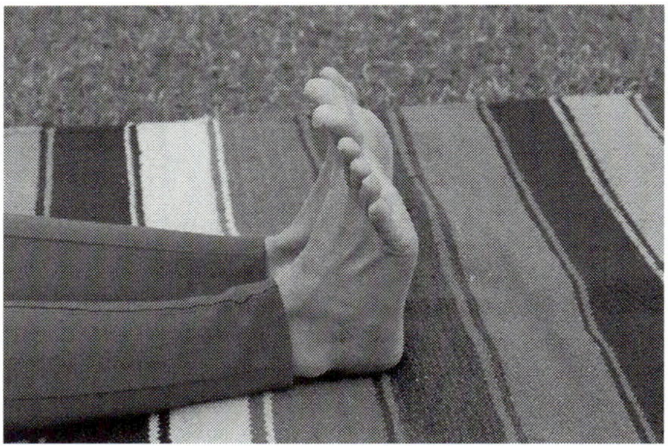

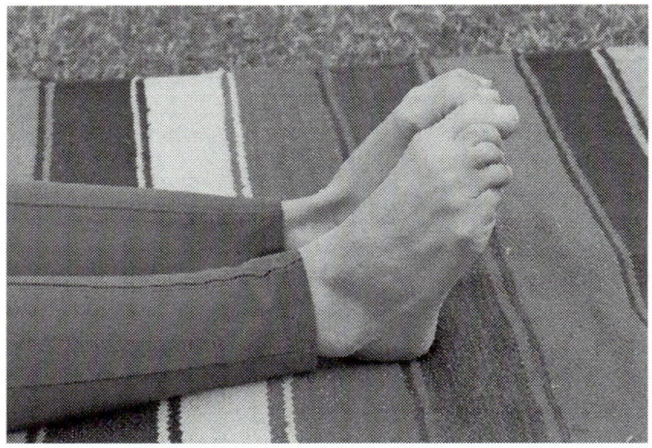

Instructions:

- Sit in Daṇḍāsana (starting position) with legs outstretched, feet together
- Place your hands slightly behind the buttocks
- Keep the spine in an erect position
- Bend the toes forwards slowly and hold for a few seconds
- Bend the toes backwards slowly towards you and hold for a few seconds
- Repeat ten times and relax

⚠ **Caution:**

Do not bend the toes with force to the point of discomfort.

✓ **Effects & Benefits:**

Strengthens the toes and associated muscles and increases circulation.

I-2 Gūlpha Naman (Ankle bending)

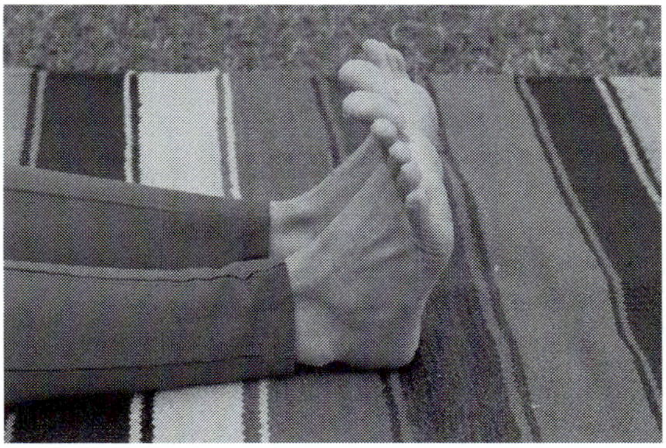

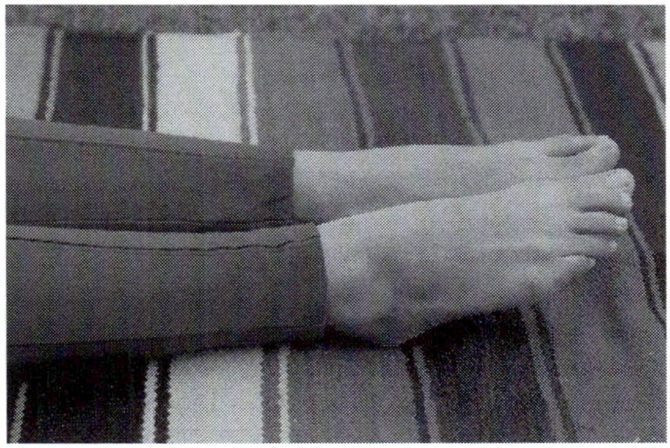

Instructions:

- Sit in Daṇḍāsana āsana
- Stretch your ankles forward and hold for a few seconds, then stretch it back and hold for a few seconds
- Repeat ten times
- Feel the stretch at all the associated muscles and joints

⚠ Caution:

Avoid jerky movements

Avoid these movements in case of any pain in ankle joints.

✓ Effects & Benefits:

Strengthens ankle joints, calves and leg muscles and improves overall flexibility of the legs.

I-3 Gūlpha Cakra (Ankle Rotation)

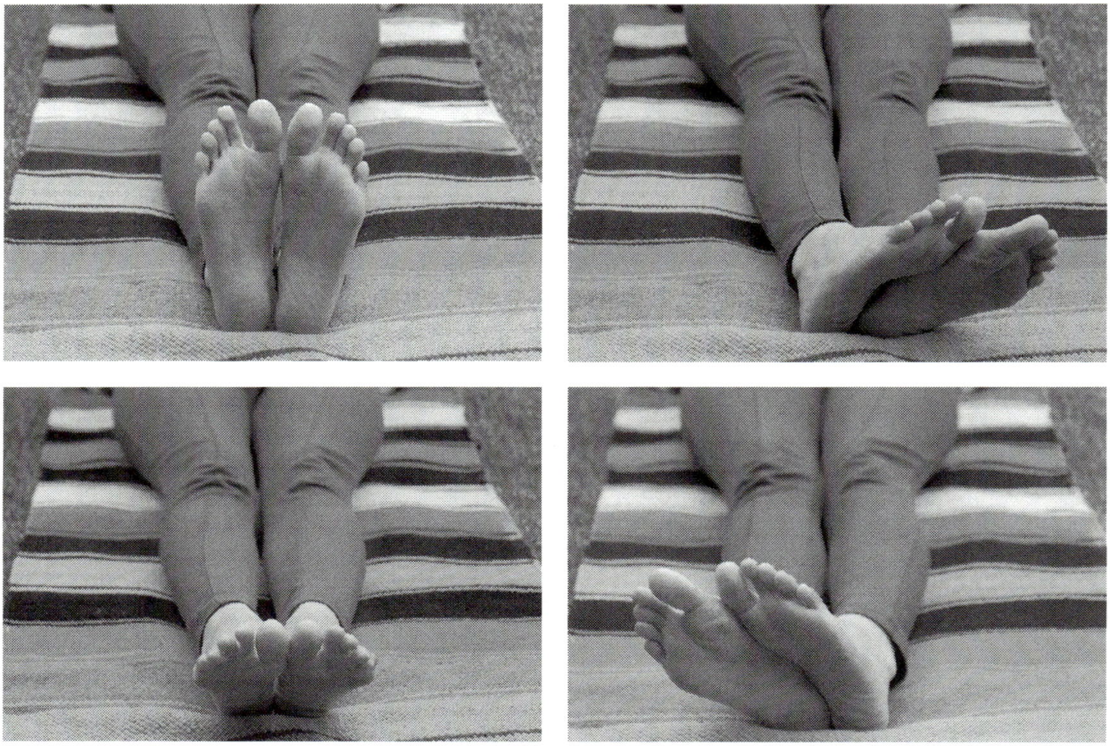

Instructions:

- Sit in Daṇḍāsana
- Slowly rotate ankles together in clockwise direction without bending the knees
- Do ten times clockwise and ten times anti-clockwise
- Relax the body keeping the feet slightly apart

⚠ **Caution:**

Rotate the ankle slowly with awareness. People with pain in ankle joints may do with caution.

✓ **Effects & Benefits:**

Strengthens ankle joints, calves and leg muscles and improves overall flexibility of the legs.

I-4 Ardha Pataṅgāsana (Half Butterfly)

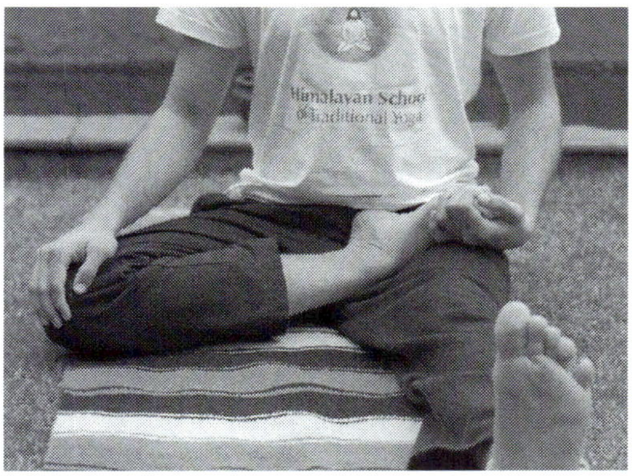

Instructions:

- Sit in Daṇḍāsana
- Place the right foot over the left thigh near the groin
- Place the right palm on top of the bent right knee.
- Hold the toes of the right foot with the left hand.
- Bring the right knee towards the floor with the help of the right hand
- Bring the right knee towards the chest and let the movements be automatic
- Repeat ten times
- Repeat same movement on the other side

⚠ **Caution:**
People with stiff hips should practice with caution.

✓ **Effects & Benefits:**
Makes hip joints more flexible and improves circulation in the hip joints.

I-5 Śroṇī Cakra (Hip-socket joint rotation)

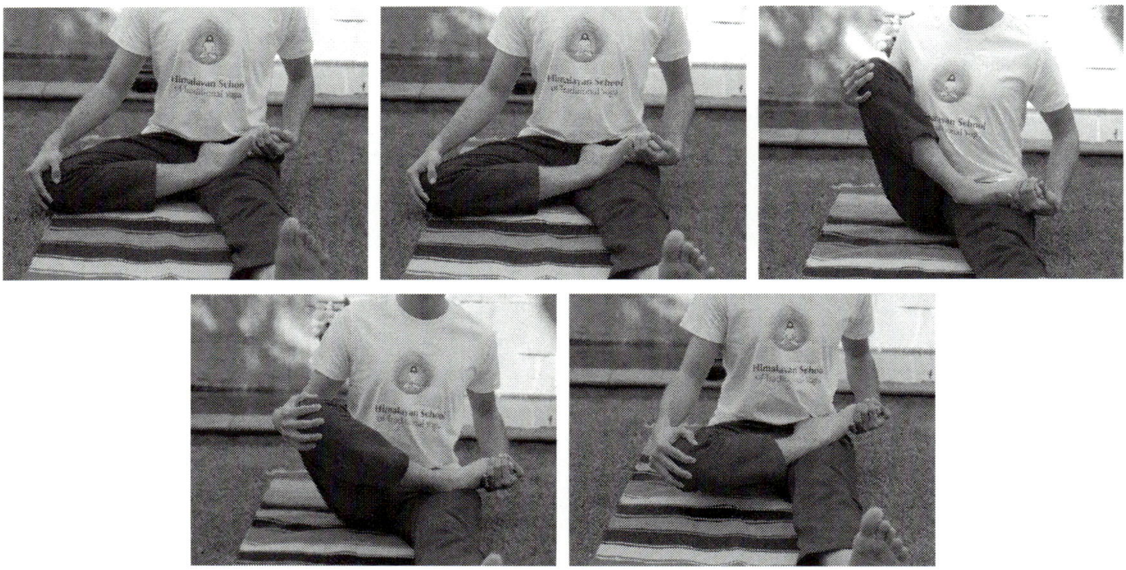

Instructions:

- Sit in Daṇḍāsana
- Place the right foot over the left thigh near to the groin
- Place the right palm on top of the bent right knee
- Hold the toes of the right foot with the left hand
- Rotate the right knee in clockwise direction with the help of the right hand
- Do the movements ten times clockwise and ten times anticlockwise
- Repeat on the other side

⚠ **Caution:**

People with hip joint pain or hip degeneration may avoid this practice.

✓ **Effects & Benefits:**

Helps in strengthening the hip joints and associated muscles and improves flexibility and circulation.

I-6 Pūrṇa Pataṅgāsana (Full-Butterfly) Variation – 1

Instructions:

- Sit in Daṇḍāsana
- Bring the soles of the feet together and clasp the hands around the toes
- Bring the heels towards the perineum
- Flap your thighs up and down in rhythmic movements
- Keep your back straight
- Repeat the movement as many times as comfortable
- Relax by straightening the legs

⚠ **Caution:**

Do not round your shoulders. People with sciatica and hip joint disorders may avoid this practice.

✓ **Effects & Benefits:**

Removes stiffness of the hips and opens up the hips area. Strengthens the hip joints and improves circulation.

I-6a Pūrṇa Pataṅgāsana (Full-Butterfly) Variation – 2

Instructions:

- Sit in Daṇḍāsana
- Bring the soles of the feet towards the perineum
- Place your palms on the knees
- Gently push the knees down with the help of the palms towards the floor
- Slowly bring the knees up to the starting position
- Repeat ten times
- Relax by straightening the legs

⚠ Caution:

Do not round the shoulders or push the knees down forcefully. People with sciatica and hip joint disorders may avoid this practice.

✓ Effects & Benefits:

Removes stiffness of the hips and opens up the hip area. Strengthens the hip joints and improves circulation.

I-7 Maṇibandhaśakti (Wrist Rotation)

Instructions:

- Stand in Samasthiti
- Keep the back straight
- Extend both the arms in front making fists with the thumbs inside
- Keep the arms straight at shoulder level
- Rotate the fists together ten times each in clockwise and anticlockwise direction
- Bring the arms down and relax

⚠ Caution:

People with cervical issues may practice cautiously.

✓ Effects & Benefits:

Relieves stress around wrists and helps in strengthening the wrist joints and carpal muscles.

I-8 Kara Pṛṣtha/Maṇibandha śakti (Back of the hand /Wrist bending/movement)

Instructions:

- Stand in Samasthiti
- Keep the back straight
- Extend both the arms in front making fists with the thumbs inside
- Keep the arms straight at shoulder level
- Bend the fists up and down
- Practice ten times
- Bring the arms down and relax

⚠ Caution:

People with pain in the wrist joints may practice cautiously.

✓ Effects & Benefits:

Relieves stress around wrists and helps in strengthening the wrist joints and carpal muscles.

I-9 Karatalaśakti (Developing palms/Palms Bending)

Instructions:

- Stand in Samasthiti
- Keep the back straight
- Keep the palms open and fingers straight throughout the entire practice.
- Bend the hands backward from the wrist as if pressing the arms against a wall, keeping the fingers pointing towards the ceiling.
- Bend the hands forward from the wrist so that the fingers point towards the floor.
- Keep the elbows straight during the whole practice.
- Do not bend the fingers.
- Repeat seven times.
- Breathing should be normal during exercise and awareness on the mental counting, movement in the wrist joints and stretching of the forearm muscles

⚠ **Caution:**

People with pain in the wrist joints may practice cautiously.

✓ **Effects & Benefits:**

Relieves stress around wrists and helps in strengthening the wrist joints and carpal muscles.

I-10 Aṅgulīmūlaśakti (Strengthening finger joints)

Instructions:

- Stand in Samasthiti
- Keep the back straight
- Extend both arms in front with palms facing outward and upward
- Keep the arms straight at shoulder level
- Bend the fingers forward and backward, up and down keeping the fingers straight
- The arm should be relaxed throughout the practice
- Repeat ten times
- Bring the arms down and relax

⚠ Caution:

People with wrist joint/carpal bone discomfort should practice the movements slowly.

✓ Effects & Benefits:

Relieves stress around wrists and helps in strengthening the wrist joints and carpal muscles and fingers.

I-11 Aṅgulīśakti (Strengthening fingers)

Instructions:

- Stand in Samasthiti
- Keep the back straight
- Extend both the arms in front at shoulder level
- Shape the fingers like the hood of a cobra and stiffen the arms
- Pull the hands towards the shoulders with resistance
- Repeat the movement ten times
- Bring the arms down and relax

⚠ Caution:

Do not apply undue force while bringing the arms towards the shoulders.

✓ Effects & Benefits:

Strengthens the wrists, palms, fingers and finger joints.

I-12 Kūrparanamanam (Elbow bending)

Instructions:

- Stand in Samasthiti
- Keep the back straight
- Extend both the arms in front at shoulder level
- Keep the palms facing up
- Bend the arms at the elbows to bring hands towards the shoulders
- Stretch the arms back palms facing up to shoulder level
- Repeat the movement ten times
- Bring the arms down and relax

⚠ **Caution:**

Avoid if pain or discomfort in elbows or shoulder joints.

✓ **Effects & Benefits:**

Removes stiffness of the elbow joints, strengthens the elbows and upper arms.

I-13 Skandhamūlaśakti (Shoulder root strengthening)

Instructions:

- Stand in Samasthiti
- Keep the back straight
- Extend both the arms in front at shoulder level
- Bend the right arm at the elbow to place fingers on the right shoulder
- Slowly rotate the right elbow in a large circle, ten times clockwise and ten times anti-clockwise
- Repeat the practice on the left side
- Maintain a straight posture throughout the practice
- Bring the arms down and relax

⚠ **Caution:**

Avoid if pain or discomfort in elbows or shoulder joints.

✓ **Effects & Benefits:**

Removes stiffness of shoulder joints, strengthens the shoulders and upper back.

I-14 Skandha uthana śakti (Shoulder stretch)

Instructions:

- Stand in Samasthiti
- Keep the back straight
- Extend both the arms above the head
- Bend the right arm at the elbow to place the right hand on the left shoulder. Right arm should stay behind the head.
- Bring the left hand to clasp the right wrist and pull the right hand towards the left shoulder. Feel the stretch in the right upper arm and right arm pit.
- Maintain the stretch for a few seconds
- Repeat on the other side
- Do the practice 3 times
- Maintain erect spine
- Bring the arms down and relax

⚠ Caution:

People with disorders of shoulders and neck may avoid this practice.

✓ Effects & Benefits:

Strengthens the shoulders and associated muscles and removes stiffness of the neck.

I-15 Skandha Cakra (Shoulder rotation)

Instructions:

- Stand in Samasthiti
- Keep the back straight
- Extend both the arms in front at shoulder level
- Bend the arms at the elbows to bring fingers towards the respective shoulders
- Slowly rotate the elbows in a large circle, ten times clockwise and ten times anti-clockwise
- Maintain a straight posture throughout the practice
- Bring the arms down and relax

⚠ **Caution:**

Avoid if pain or discomfort in elbow or shoulder joints .

✓ **Effects & Benefits:**

Removes stiffness of the shoulder joints, strengthens the shoulders and upper back.

I-16 Grīvaśakti (Neck movements)

Variation – 1

Instructions:

- Stand in Samasthiti
- Keep the back straight
- Keep the shoulders relaxed and gaze straight ahead
- Gently turn the head to the right with the chin towards the right shoulder
- Maintain the position for a few seconds
- Slowly turn the head to the left side with chin towards the left shoulder
- Maintain the position for a few seconds
- Bring the head to the centre and relax
- Repeat the practice 5 times

⚠ Caution:

People with neck discomfort, pain, or cervical disorders may avoid the practice.

✓ Effects & Benefits:

Removes stiffness around the neck, strengthens the neck muscles and improves circulation in neck region.

I-16a Grīvaśakti (Neck movements)

Variation – 2

Instructions:

- Stand in Samasthiti
- Keep the back straight
- Keep the shoulders relaxed and gaze straight ahead
- Bring the head forward and try to touch the chin to the chest
- Maintain the position for a few seconds
- Move the head up and back as much as comfortable
- Maintain the position for a few seconds
- Feel the stretch in the front and back of the neck
- Practice five times
- Bring the head back to normal position and relax

⚠ **Caution:**

People with neck discomfort, pain, vertigo, or cervical disorders may avoid the practice.

✓ **Effects & Benefits:**

Removes stiffness around the neck, strengthens the neck muscles and improves circulation in neck region.

I-17 Grīvacakra (Neck rotation)

Variation – 3

Instructions:

- Stand in Samasthiti
- Keep the back straight
- Keep the shoulders relaxed and gaze straight ahead
- Gently bring the head down and rotate first to the right clockwise and then anticlockwise very slowly
- Repeat the practice five times
- If there is any discomfort, avoid the practice.
- Bring the head to normal position and relax

⚠ **Caution:**

People with neck discomfort, pain, vertigo, or cervical disorders should avoid the practice.

✓ **Effects & Benefits:**

Removes stiffness around the neck, strengthens the neck muscles and improves circulation in the neck region.

I-18 Netraśakti (Eye movements)
Variation – 1

Instructions:
- Sit in any comfortable position of choice or in half lotus posture
- Keep the back and neck straight
- Keeping the eyes open, look towards the right and hold for a few seconds
- Turn the eyes to the left and hold for a few seconds
- Repeat the practice five times
- Close and relax the eyes for a few seconds

⚠ **Caution:**
Avoid the practice in case of any eye infections. Only eyeballs should move left and right and not the head or face.

✓ **Effects & Benefits:**
Strengthens the eye muscles andnerves, helps to improve vision.

I-18a Netraśakti (Eye movements)

Variation – 2

Instructions:

- Sit in any comfortable position of choice or in half lotus posture
- Keep the back and neck straight
- Keeping the eyes open, look up and hold for a few seconds
- Turn the eyeballs down and hold for a few seconds
- Repeat the practice five times
- Close and relax the eyes for a few seconds

⚠ **Caution:**

Avoid the practice in case of any eye infections. Only eyeballs should move up and down and not the head or face.

✓ **Effects & Benefits:**

Strengthens the eye muscles andnerves, helps to improve vision.

I-19 Dṛṣṭicakra (Eye Rotation)

Variation – 3

Instructions:

- Sit in any comfortable position of choice or in half lotus posture
- Keep the back and neck straight
- Keeping the eyes open rotate the eyeballs clockwise and anti-clockwise five times each
- Close and relax the eyes for a few seconds

⚠ **Caution:**

Avoid the practice in case of any eye infections. Only eyeballs should rotate and not the head or face.

✓ **Effects & Benefits:**

Strengthens the eye muscles andnerves, helps to improve vision.

I-20 Bhrūmadhyadṛṣti (Eye gazing at centre of eyebrows)

Instructions:

- Sit in a comfortable position or half lotus posture
- Keep the back and neck straight
- Gently lift the eyes to look between the eyebrows
- Breathing should be normal and awareness should be at the centre of eyebrows

⚠ **Caution:**

Do not overstrain the eye muscles, or forehead while fixing the gaze. People with headache, or migraines should avoid the practice.

✓ **Effects & Benefits:**

Helps in calming the mind and builds concentration.

I-21 Nāsikāgradṛṣti (Eye gazing at the tip of nose)

Instructions:

- Sit in a comfortable position or half lotus posture
- Keep the back and neck straight
- Gently bring the eyes to focus at the tip of nose
- Breathing should be normal and awareness should be at the tip of the nose

⚠ **Caution:**

Do not overstrain the eye muscles, or forehead while fixing the gaze. People with headache, or migraines should avoid the practice.

✓ **Effects & Benefits:**

Helps in calming the mind and builds concentration.

I-22 Netramardanam (Eye Pressing)

Instructions:

- Sit in a comfortable position or half lotus posture
- Keep the back and neck straight
- Keep the body relaxed and theeyes closed
- Squeeze the eye lids and close them tightly tensing the eye muscles
- Hold the squeeze for a few seconds and release
- Feel the relaxation in the eye muscles
- Repeat five times

⚠ **Caution:**

Do not overstrain the eye muscles by squeezing too tightly.

✓ **Effects & Benefits:**

Helps in releasing tension around eye muscles and relaxing them.

I-23 Hastagharṣaṇam (Palming)

Instructions:

- Sit in a comfortable position or half lotus posture
- Keep the back and neck straight
- Keep the body relaxed and the eyes closed
- Rub the palms of the hands together and generate heat between the palms
- Place the palms gently over the eye lids without any undue pressure
- Feel the warmth of the palms on the eyes and maintain for a few seconds
- Gently bring the hands down and slowly open the eyes
- Repeat this procedure a couple of times

✓ **Effects & Benefits:**

Helps in releasing tension around eye muscles, relaxing them. Alsocalms the mind.

I-24 Kapōlaśakti (Rejuvenating and strengthening cheek muscles)

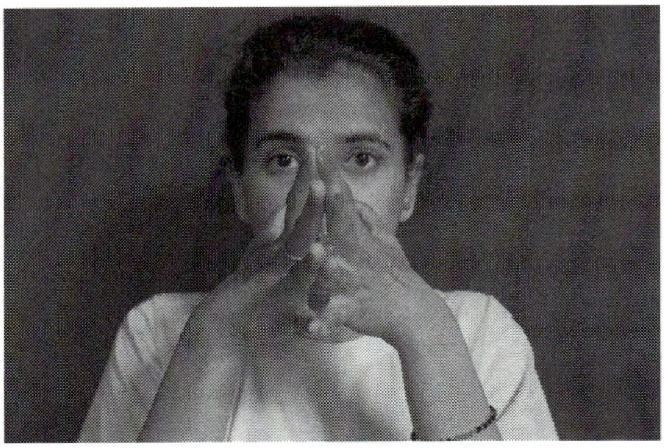

Instructions:

- Sit in a comfortable position or half lotus posture
- Keep the back and neck straight
- Keep the body relaxed and the eyes closed
- Bring the tips of fingers together and close the nostrils with the thumbs
- Suck the breath in, fill the cheeks with air and close the mouth
- Hold the air inside the mouth puffing the cheeks to create a gentle pressure in cheeks and facial muscles
- Hold for a few seconds and feel the tension in the cheeks
- Slowly release the air through the mouth by removing the hands
- Repeat five times.
- Feel the relaxation in cheeks and facial muscles

⚠ **Caution:**

Do not overstrain facial muscles or hold for too long.

Effects & Benefits:

Helps in relaxing and toning facial muscles.

I-25 Karṇaśakti (Improving Power of hearing)

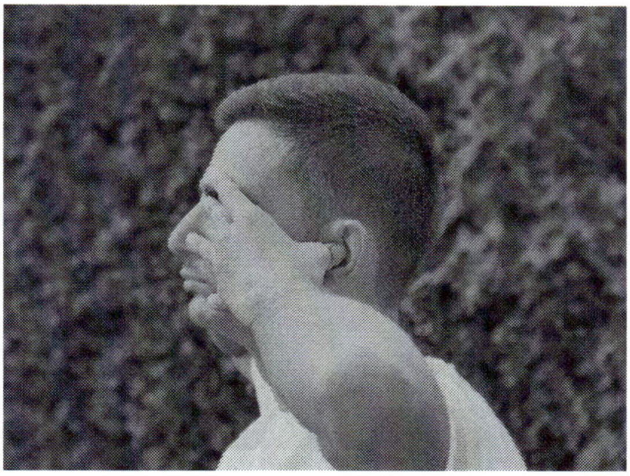

Instructions:

- Sit in a comfortable position or half lotus posture
- Keep back and neck straight
- Keep the body relaxed and theeyes closed
- Close the ears with the thumbs
- Place the index fingers on the eyes
- The middle and ring fingers shall encircle the mouth
- Keep the eyes open and shape your lips like the beak of a crow and suck in air with a hissing sound to blow out the cheeks
- Hold the breath, closing the eyes and rest the chin on the throat
- Maintain the position for a few seconds
- Open the eyes, remove the fingers, take the head back to normal position and exhale through the nose
- Repeat five times and relax

⚠ **Caution:**

Cheeks should be fully blown out while holding the breath.

✓ **Effects & Benefits:**

Helps in improving the power of hearing.

I-26 Udaraśakti (Strengthening abdomen)

Instructions:

- Stand in Samasthithi or sit in a comfortable position or half lotus posture
- Keep the back straight
- Inhale and bring the abdomen out
- Exhale and take the abdomen inside
- Squeeze the abdominal muscles tensing them
- Hold for a few seconds and slowly release
- Feel the relaxation in the abdomen
- Repeat five times and relax

⚠ **Caution:**

People who have recently undergone an abdominal surgery or are undergoing menstrual cycle should avoid this practice.

✓ **Effects & Benefits:**

Helps in massaging and strengthening the abdominal organs increasing circulation.

(Yoga Sutra 2.28)

yogângânusthânâd asuddhi-ksaye jnâna-dîptir âviveka-khyâteh

Through the practice of the different limbs of yoga, impurities are eliminated or destroyed. When each limb of the eight-limbed path is practiced, only then comes knowledge of the reality. If impediments or impurities are there, knowledge is not there. Once the impediments are removed, knowledge reveals itself culminating in discriminative wisdom
i.e. realisation of one's true nature.

(Yoga Sutra 2.29)

yama-niyamâsana-prâñâyâma-pratyâhâra-dhârañâ-dhyâna-samâdhayo'stâv angâni

The eight limbs of yoga are the codes of self-regulation or restraint, observances or practices of self-training, postures, expansion of breath and prana, withdrawal of the senses, concentration, meditation, and perfected concentration.

II Dynamic Yogic Excercisies

II-27 Rekhāgati (Walking in a straight line)

Instructions:

- Stand in Samasthithi, spine erect, hands by the sides.
- Keep the gaze straight, slightly ahead of the toes
- Walk forward in a straight line keeping the heel of one foot in front of the toe of the other
- Take a few steps in this manner, walking steadily and slowly, breathing normally, with the gaze and awareness on the ground in front
- Start walking backwards without turning back taking one step at a time, placing toe of one foot at the back of heel of the other
- Repeat the practice a couple of times

⚠ **Caution:**

People having vertigo, or giddiness have to practice with caution.

✓ **Effects & Benefits:**

Improves balance, concentration, and calms the mind.

II-28 Drdhagati (The Locomotive Walking Exercise)

Instructions:

- Stand in Samasthithi, spine erect, hands by the sides
- Push the arm forward and backward alternately in a piston like movement
- The feet are to be thrown back from the knee to hit the buttocks
- While the right leg is forward, right arm should be forward and vice versa
- Breathe through nose sharply and deeply producing the hissing sound of an engine
- Repeat the practice for a few minutes

⚠ **Caution:**

People with knee pain or shoulder pain should practice with caution, and people with heart ailments should avoid the practice.

✓ **Effects & Benefits:**

This practice helps in circulation and revitalises the entire body. It tones the arms and legs and helps in strengthening the respiratory system.

II-29 Drutagati (The Locomotive Running Exercise)

Instructions:

- Stand in Samasthithi, spine erect, hands by the sides
- Push the arm forward and backward alternately in a piston like movement
- The feet are to be thrown back from the knee to hit the buttocks
- While the right leg is forward, right arm should also be forward and vice versa
- Breathe through nose sharply and deeply producing the hissing sound of an engine
- Keeping the head straight, start running
- Run for a few minutes steadily in one place and then relax

⚠ **Caution:**

People with knee and shoulder pain should practice with caution and people with heart ailments should avoid the practice.

✓ **Effects & Benefits:**

This practice helps in circulation and revitalises the entire body. It tones the arms and legs and helps in strengthening the respiratory system.

II-30 Janghaśaktivikāsa (Thigh strengthening and arm strengthening)

Instructions:

- Stand in Samasthithi, spine erect, hands by the sides
- Jump and open the legs sideways raising the arms simultaneously to shoulder level
- Take another jump to bring back the legs and hands to starting position
- Take a few jumps, repeating the movement of legs and arms, and then relax

⚠ **Caution:**

People with knee and shoulder pain should practice with caution and people with heart ailments should avoid the practice.

✓ **Effects & Benefits:**

This practice helps in circulation and revitalises the entire body and it tones the arms and legs.

(Yoga Sutra 2.31)

ahimsâ-satyâsteya-brahmacaryâparigrahâ yamâh

Non-violence, truthfulness, abstention from stealing, continence and non-possessiveness or non-attachment are the five Yamās or codes of self-regulation. The yamās are the first of the eight rungs or limbs of Yoga. Practicing the abstinences mentioned above (Yamās), - ensures that we leave a positive mark on the world and we remain kind and compassionate to others, including other sentient beings of the world. However, this does not mean that we are passive or that we remain doormats or that we do not protect ourselves from negativity or attacks from the outside world.

III Standing Āsanas

III-1 Samasthiti (Starting Position)

Instructions:

- Sama in Sanskrit means same, Sthiti means state or position. It refers to the starting position of any Āsana
- For a standing Āsana, a Samasthiti would be to stand with feet together, knees together, hands by the sides, chin parallel to the ground
- The weight of the body should be equally distributed on both feet
- Breathing should be normal

III-2 Tādāsana : Straight Tree

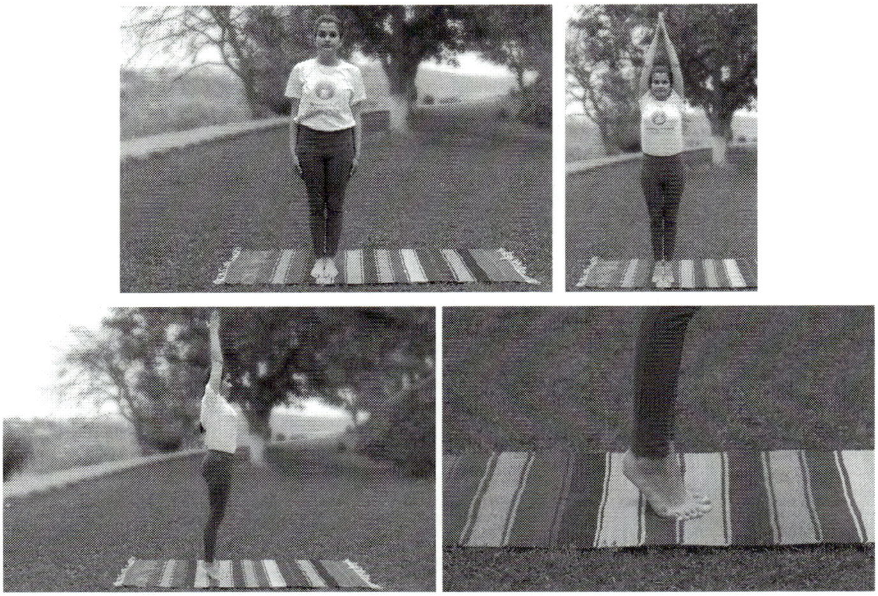

Instructions:

- Stand in Samasthiti with weight of the body equally distributed on both feet
- Inhale and slowly raise the arms from the sides to clasp hands over the head, interlocking the fingers and turning them out
- Simultaneously lift the heels off the floor
- Stay in the position, breathing normally
- Feel the stretch of the whole body from top to bottom
- Exhale, bring the heels down while simultaneously bringing the arms to the sides
- Relax before doing another round

⚠ **Caution:**

People with ankle stiffness or pain in the ankles, suffering from vertigo, low blood pressure, insomnia etc should avoid this posture.

✓ **Effects & Benefits:**

This Āsana helps in strengthening the spine, makes ankles more flexible and stronger. The muscles and ligaments of the abdominal region are stretched, helping them to function more effectively. It helps in developing physical and mental balance.

III-3a Tiryak Tādāsana: A

Instructions:

- Stand in Samasthithi, feet together, knees together, hands by the sides, chin down
- The weight of the body should be equally distributed on both feet
- Inhale, slowly raise arms from the sides to clasp hands overhead, interlocking the fingers and turning the palms outward, simultaneously lifting the heels off the floor
- Exhale, twist the torso to the right
- Inhale, come back to the centre
- Exhale, twist the torso to the left
- Inhale, come back to the centre
- Exhale, bring the heels and arms down
- Relax before doing another round

⚠ **Caution:**

People with ankle stiffness or pain in the ankles, lower back pain, suffering from vertigo, low blood pressure, insomnia etc should avoid this posture.

✓ **Effects & Benefits:**

This Āsana helps in strengthening the spine, makes the ankles more flexible and stronger. The muscles and ligaments of the abdominal region are stretched, helping them to function effectively. It helps in developing physical and mental balance.

III-3b Tiryak Tādāsana: B (Swaying Tree posture)

Instructions:

- Stand with feet apart, hands by the sides
- Inhale raising the arms up to interlock fingers, turning palms up
- Exhale and bend to the right from the waist
- Breathe normally and stay in the position
- Inhale and straighten, bringing the arms up
- Exhale and bend to the left from the waist
- Breathe normally and stay in the position
- Inhale and straighten, bringing the arms up
- Exhale and bring the arms down to sides

⚠ **Caution:**

Beginners should not hold the posture for too long.

✓ **Effects & Benefits:**

Stretches the spine, strengthens abdominal muscles and ligaments, stretches and makes the waist slim.

III-4 Katicakrāsana: A (Waist twisting posture)

Instructions:

- Stand with the feet shoulder width apart, arms by the sides
- Inhale, raise the arms to shoulder level
- Exhale, twist from the waist to the right keeping the right arm straight and left arm bent at the elbow
- Stay in the position, breathing normally
- Inhale, bring the arms to shoulder level
- Exhale, twist from the waist to the left keeping the left arm straight and right arm bent at the elbow
- Stay in the position, breathing normally
- Inhale, bring the arms to shoulder level
- Exhale, bring the arms down to the sides

⚠ **Caution:**

People with Spinal disorders, hernia, and abdominal issues should avoid this posture.

✓ **Effects & Benefits:**

This Āsana helps in strengthening the spine, makes the waist slim, and strengthens the arms, neck, shoulders and abdominal region.

III-4a Katicakrāsana: B (Waist twisting posture)

Instructions:

- Stand with feet shoulder width apart, arms by the sides
- Inhale, raise the arms to shoulder level.
- Exhale, twist from the waist to the right placing the left hand on the right shoulder taking the right arm around the back to place the back of the right hand on the left side of the waist
- Stay in the position and breathe normally
- Inhale, bring the arms to shoulder level
- Exhale, twist from the waist to the left placing the right hand on the left shoulder taking the left arm around the back to place the back of the left hand on the right side of the waist
- Stay in the position and breathe normally
- Inhale, bring the arms to shoulder level
- Exhale, bring the arms down to the sides

⚠ **Caution:**
People with Spinal disorders, hernia, abdominal issues etc. should avoid this posture.

✓ **Effects & Benefits:**
This Āsana strengthens the spine, neck, arms, shoulders, abdomen, and makes the waist slim and supple.

III-4b Katicakrāsana: C (Lateral bend from the waist)

Instructions:

- Stand with feet shoulder width apart, arms by the sides
- Inhale, raise left arm to shoulder level
- Turn the left palm up
- Exhale, bend from the waist to the right laterally, raising the left arm over the head so that the left upper arm is close to the left ear
- Stay in the position and breathe normally
- Inhale, bring the torso up to the centre simultaneously bringing the left arm up to shoulder level palm facing up
- Exhale, turn the palms down bringing the arm down to the sides
- Repeat on the other side

Note: Initially one can keep the feet apart and practice. After attaining flexibility, keep the feet together.

⚠ **Caution:**
People with spinal disorders, hernia, abdominal issues etc. should avoid this posture.

✓ **Effects & Benefits:**
This Āsana strengthens the spine, neck, arms, shoulders, abdomen, and makes the waist slim and supple.

III-5 Trikoṇāsana (Triangle posture) Lateral

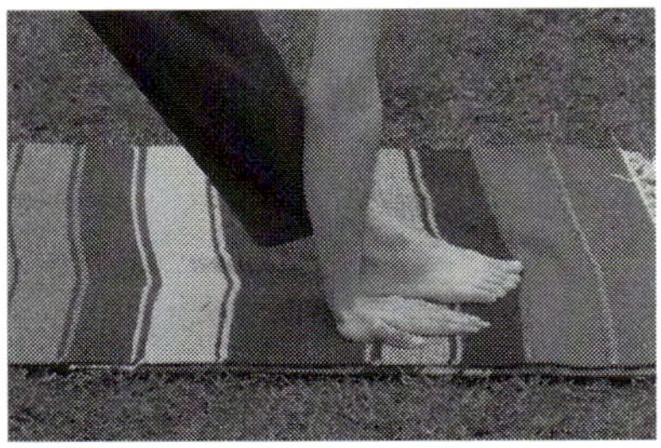

Instructions:

- Stand in Samasthiti
- Take a big step sideways
- Turn the right foot outwards
- Inhale, raise the arms to shoulder level
- Exhale and bend the torso laterally to the right to place the right hand besides the right foot, keeping the left arm straight above the head
- Turn the head to look up at the raised left arm.
- Stay in the position and breathe normally
- Inhale andcome up to the centre position with the arms raised to shoulder level
- Exhale and bring the arms down to the sides
- Repeat on the other side

Note: Initially one can keep the feet straight and practice Trikonāsana both lateral and twist. Later when one is more flexible, one can turn the foot outwards.

⚠ Caution:

People with vertigo, high /low blood pressure, heart problem should avoid this Āsana. People with back & neck problem should practice caution.

✓ Effects & Benefits:

This Āsana improves body balance, strengthens feet, ankles and legs. It helps in stretching and toning calves, hamstring muscles and waist. The arms, neck, and shoulders are strengthened.

III-5a Trikoṇāsana (Parivrtti) (Triangle posture) (Twist)

Instructions:

- Stand in Samasthiti
- Take a big step sideways
- Turn the right foot outwards
- Inhale and raise the arms to shoulder level
- Exhale and bend the torso forward from the hips to twist to the right placing left hand besides right foot
- Turn the head to look up at the raised right arm
- Stay in the position and breathe normally
- Inhale and come up to the centre position with the arms raised to the shoulder level
- Exhale andbring arms down to sides
- Repeat on the other side

Note: Initially one can keep the feet straight and practice Trikonāsana,both lateral and twist. Later when one is more flexible, one can turn the foot outwards.

⚠ **Caution:**
People with knee, ankle, back and neck disorders may avoid this practice.

✓ **Effects & Benefits:**
This Āsana helps in strengthening the abdominal muscles and organs and improves the digestive system.

III-6 Vṛkṣāsana (Tree posture)

Instructions:

- Stand in Samasthiti
- Balancing the body weight on the left leg, lift the right foot to place the sole of the right foot on the left groin
- Inhale, raise the arms up to join the palms in prayer position above the head
- Fix the gaze on a particular point at a distance
- Stay in the position and breathe normally
- Exhale, bring the arms down to the sides
- Bring the left foot down and relax
- Repeat on the other side

⚠ Caution:

People with weak knees, vertigo, giddiness etc. may avoid the posture.

✓ Effects & Benefits:

This Āsana helps to improve concentration, body balance and alignment. It Improves the neuro muscular coordination.

III-7 Pranāmāsana (Prayer posture)

Instructions:

- Stand in Samasthiti
- Inhale, raise the arms to chest level
- Join both the palms in prayer posture
- Stay in the position and breathe normally
- Exhale, bring the arms down to the sides

✓ **Effects & Benefits:**

Makes the mind calm

III-8 Hasta Uthānāsana (Hand raising posture)

Instructions:

- Stand in Samasthiti
- Inhale, raising the arms over the head
- Push the chest out and arch the back
- Stay in the position and breathe normally
- Exhale and bring the arms down to the sides

⚠ **Caution:**

People with dizziness, vertigo, cervical problem, high blood pressure/low blood pressure, to practise slowly without overstraining.

Effects & Benefits:

This Āsana helps in expanding the chest and improves lung capacity.

III-9 Pādahastāsana (Hands to feet posture)

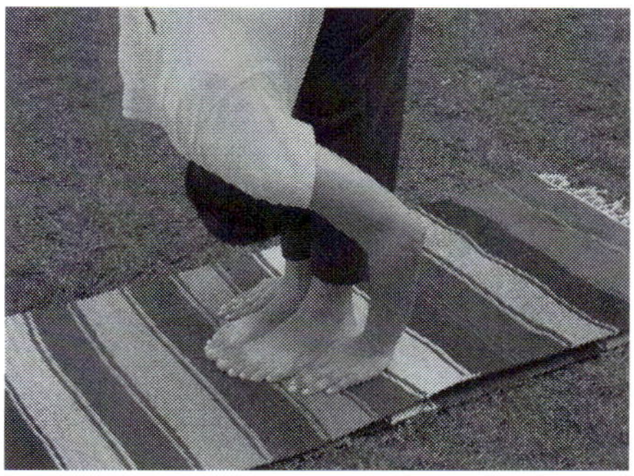

Instructions:

- Stand in Samasthiti
- Inhale, raise the arms from the front
- Keep the chest out and back arched
- Exhale, bend forward from the hips to place the hands besides feet
- The forehead should be touching the knees
- Stay in the position and breathe normally
- Inhale, come up slowly raising the hands up
- Exhale, bring the arms down to the sides

⚠ **Caution:**

People suffering from back problems, sciatica, hypertension, vertigo, knee and heart problems, should avoid this posture.

✓ **Effects & Benefits:**

This Āsana helps in effective functioning of the abdominal muscles and organs and aids in digestion. It strengthens the hamstrings, spine and back.

III-10 Uthānāsana: Upward Extension Posture

Instructions:

- Stand in Samasthithi
- Inhale, raise the arms from the front
- Exhale, bend forward from the hips to place the hands beyond the feet, forehead touching knees or beyond knees
- Relax the neck and arms in the final position
- Stay in the position breathing normally
- Inhale, come up slowly raising the arms up
- Exhale and bring arms down to the sides

Note: This āsana is a more advanced version of Padahastāsana

⚠ **Caution:**

People with spinal disorders, back pain, cervical spondylitis, Vertigo, and Hypertension should avoid this posture.

✓ **Effects & Benefits:**

This Āsana strengthens the hamstring muscles, makes spine flexible, improves digestion, removes constipation, and enhances blood flow to the head region.

III-11 Aśva sañchalanāsana (Equestrian posture)

Instructions:
- Stand in Samasthiti
- Inhale, raise the arms up from the front, keeping the chest out and the back arched
- Exhale, bend forward from the hips to place the hands besides the feet
- Touch the forehead to the knees
- Inhale, stretch the right leg back bending the left knee, keeping the left foot on the floor in between the hands
- Breathe normally
- Exhale and bring the right foot forward to Padahastāsana position.
- Repeat on the left side
- Relax in Samasthiti

⚠ Caution:
Persons with knee, ankles, back joint disorders and hernia should avoid this posture.

✓ Effects & Benefits:
This Āsana strengthens the abdominal organs and improves their functioning. It strengthens the thigh and legs muscles.

III-12 Parvatāsana (Mountain posture)

Instructions:

- Stand in Samasthiti
- Inhale, raise the arms up from the front, keeping the chest out and the back arched
- Exhale, bend forward from the hips to place the hands besides the feet
- Touch the forehead to the knees
- Inhale, stretch the right leg back bending the left knee keeping the left foot on the floor in between the hands
- Exhale, bring the left foot back besides the right foot
- Push the feet down to the floor, raise the hips and bring the head down between the arms
- Keep the legs and arms straight, and theheels firmly on the floor
- Stay in the position breathing normally
- Inhale, bring the left foot forward to Ashwa Sanchalanāsana
- Exhale, and come to Padahastāsana
- Inhale, and come to Hasta Uttanāsana
- Exhale, bring the arms down to the sides and relax in Samasthiti

⚠ Caution:

People with shoulder, arms and knee pain should practice with caution.

✓ Effects & Benefits:

This Āsana helps in expansion of the chest region. The arms, neck, shoulders, legs and abdominal regions are strengthened.

III-13 Aṛdhacandrāsana (Half Moon posture)

Instructions:

- Stand in Samasthiti
- Inhale, raise the arms up from the front, keeping the chest out andtheback arched
- Exhale, bend forward from the hips to place the hands besides the feet
- Touch the forehead to the knees
- Inhale, stretch the right leg back bending the left knee, keeping the left foot on the floor in between the hands
- Exhale in this position
- Inhale, raise the arms and bring the palms together, arch the back, push the chest forward and look up
- There should be a curve from the tips of the fingers to the tips of the toes resembling a crescent moon
- Stay in the posture, breathing normally
- Exhale, bring the arms down to place them besides the feet
- Repeat on the other side
- Then come back to Padahastāsana, Hastauttanāsana and back to Samasthiti

Note: This posture is also referred as Anjeneyāsana

⚠ **Caution:**

People with vertigo, knee problems, and cervical issues should avoid this posture.

✓ **Effects & Benefits:**

This Āsana helps in expansion of the chest region. The arms, neck, shoulders and abdominal region are strengthened.

III-14 Pārśva Uthānāsana: Lateral Upward Extension Posture

Instructions:
- Stand in Samasthithi
- Take a big step forward with the right leg
- Turn the left foot outward, straighten the torso and ensure both the legs are straight, ensuring that the knees are straight
- Inhale, raise the arms from the front
- Exhale, bend forward from the hips to place the hands on either side of the right foot
- Touch the forehead to the knees
- Stay in the position breathing normally
- Inhale and come up slowly raising the arms up
- Exhale, bring the arms down to the sides
- Repeat on the left side

⚠ **Caution:**
People with spinal disorders, back pain, neck pain, knee joint problems, blood pressure, and Vertigo should avoid this posture.

✓ **Effects & Benefits:**
This Āsana strengthens the spine, neck, tones abdominal organs and muscles, blood circulation is improved, removes body stiffness to make it more flexible.

III-15 Prasārita Pāda Uthānāsana: Spread Leg Upward Extension Posture

Instructions:

- Stand in Samasthithi
- Take a big step sideways, with the feet 3 to 4 feet apart
- Inhale, raise the arms from the front
- Exhale, bend forward from the hips to place hands on the floor in line with the feet keeping the crown of the head on the floor in between the palms
- Stay in the position breathing normally
- Inhale, slowly come up raising the arms from the front
- Exhale, bring the arms down to the sides

⚠ **Caution:**

People with spinal disorders, back pain, neck pain, knee joint problems, high blood pressure, and vertigo should avoid this posture.

✓ **Effects & Benefits:**

This Āsana improves digestion. Abdominal organs and muscles are toned and strengthened, blood circulation is improved, and excess fat is reduced.

III-16 Ardha Utkatāsana: Halfway Squat Posture

Instructions:

- Stand in Samasthithi
- Inhale, raise the arms from the front
- Exhale, bend the knees to bring the torso halfway down, keeping the thighs parallel to the floor
- Stay in the posture breathing normally
- Inhale and come up straightening the torso
- Exhale and bring arms down to the sides

Note: After a few days of practice one can do the posture with palms together in prayer position, or palms interlocked and turned up.

⚠ **Caution:**

People with knee pain, weak ankle joints, back pain etc. should avoid this posture.

✓ **Effects & Benefits:**

This Āsana removes stiffness in shoulders & legs, strengthens knees, tones and strengthens the abdomen and helps in digestion.

III-17 Ardha Uttānāsana: Halfway Upward Extension Posture

Instructions:

- Stand in Samasthithi
- Inhale, raise the arms up from the front
- Exhale, bend forward from the hips halfway
- Keep the arms across the ears with the palms facing down
- Inhale and arch the back
- Exhale and relax the back
- Stay in the position taking a couple of breaths
- Inhale, come up raising the arms from the front
- Exhale, bringing the arms down to the sides

⚠ **Caution:**

People with back pain, cervical spondylitis, vertigo, and hypertension may avoid this posture.

✓ **Effects & Benefits:**

This Āsana strengthens hamstring muscles, makes spine flexible, and improves digestion.

III-18 Utkatāsana: Squat Posture

Instructions:

- Stand in Samasthithi
- Inhale, raise the arms up from the front
- Exhale, bend the knees and squat down, feet firmly on the ground, keeping the back straight
- Stay in the posture breathing normally
- Inhale and come up raising the arms from the front
- Exhale and bring the arms down to the sides

⚠ **Caution:**

People having knee pain, weak ankle joints, back pain etc. should avoid this posture.

✓ **Effects & Benefits:**

Āsana remove stiffness and strengthens shoulders & legs. Respiratory diaphragm and abdominal organs are toned and strengthened.

III-19 Vīrabhadrāsana - 1 (Warrior posture)

Instructions:

- Stand in Samasthiti
- Take a big step forward with the right leg
- Turn the left foot outwards, straighten the torso to the centre
- Inhale, raise the arms from the front simultaneously bending the right knee
- Thigh should be parallel to the ground
- Extend arms above the head, keeping the palms together
- Stay in the position breathing normally
- Exhale and bring hands down to the sides simultaneously straightening the right leg
- Bring the right foot back to starting position
- Repeat on the left side

⚠ **Caution:**

People with hernia, knee and back pain, spinal disorders etc should avoid the posture.

✓ **Effects & Benefits:**

This Āsana helps in expansion of the chest region. It strengthens the arms, neck, shoulders and knees.

III-19 Vīrabhadrāsana - 2:

Instructions:

- Stand in Samasthithi
- Take a big step sideways, with the legs three to four feet apart
- Turn the right foot outwards, keeping the left foot straight
- Inhale, raise arms to the shoulder level with the palms facing down
- Exhale, bend the right knee, keeping thigh parallel to the floor
- Turn the head to the right to gaze at the right hand
- Stay in the posture breathing normally
- Inhale, straightening the right knee bringing head to the centre
- Exhale and bring the arms down to the sides
- Repeat on the left side

⚠ Caution:

People with weak ankles, knees, cervical problems, and spinal disorders may avoid this posture.

Effects & Benefits:

This Āsana removes stiffness and strengthens legs, arms, knees and back. It tones the abdominal organs and muscles.

III-19 Vīrabhadrāsana - 3:

Instructions:

- Stand in Samasthithi
- Take a big step forward with the right leg
- Turn the left foot slightly outward and straighten the torso
- Inhale, raise the arms from the front, bending the right knee whilearching the back and keeping the palms together
- Exhale and move forward, straightening the right knee and simultaneously lifting the left leg off the floor
- Keep the right leg straight and vertical
- The whole body, arms and left leg should be parallel to the floor
- Focus the eyes on the palms
- Stay in the posture breathing normally
- Inhale, lower the left leg to the floor, bending the right knee bringing the arms up and arching the back
- Exhale, straighten the right knee and bring the arms down to the sides
- Repeat on the other side

⚠ **Caution:**

People with high blood pressure, vertigo, weak knee joints etc should avoid this posture.

✓ **Effects & Benefits:**

This Āsana removes stiffness, strengthens arms, makes back flexible and strong and tones the abdomen.

III-20 Pārśvakōnāsana Uthitha: Lateral Standing Angled Posture

Instructions:

- Stand in Samasthithi
- Take a big step sideways legs apart about three to four feet
- Turn the right foot outward
- Inhale, raise the arms from the sides to shoulder level with the palms facing down
- Exhale, bend the right knee moving the torso laterally to place the right palm outside the right foot
- Extend the left arm and turn the head to look up at the left palm
- Inhale and bring the left arm across the right ear
- Stay in the position breathing normally
- Exhale and straighten the left arm back to the vertical position
- Inhale, turn the head to the centre and come up straightening the right leg
- Exhale and bring the arms down to the sides
- Repeat on the other side

⚠ **Caution:**

People with high blood pressure, cardiac problems, weak knee joints, back pain etc should avoid the posture.

✓ **Effects & Benefits:**

This Āsana expands the thorax, strengthens knees, thighs, prevents back pain, and stimulates intestinal peristalsis.

III-20 A Pārśvakōnāsana (Parivrtti): Lateral Angled Posture – Twist

Instructions:

- Stand in Samasthithi
- Take a big step sideways, legs about three to four feet apart
- Turn the right foot outward
- Inhale, raise the arms from the sides to shoulder level with the palms facing down
- Exhale, bend the right knee and twist to the right to place the left hand on the floor outside the right foot
- Extend the right arm up, turn the head to look up at the right palm
- Inhale and bring the right arm across the left ear
- Stay in the position breathing normally
- Exhale and straighten the right arm back to the vertical position
- Inhale, turn the head to the centre and come up straightening the right leg
- Exhale and bring the arms down to the sides
- Repeat on the other side

⚠ **Caution:**

People with high blood pressure, cardiac problems, spinal disorders, weak knee joints etc should avoid this posture.

✓ **Effects & Benefits:**

This Āsana expands the thorax, strengthens knees, thighs, prevents back pain, and stimulates the digestive system.

III-21 Natrajāsana: Lord of Dance Posture

Instructions:

- Stand in Samasthithi
- Raise the left arm from the front keeping it parallel to the flooFor beginners or intermediate practitioners :
- Bend the right knee and lift the leg up
- Hold the right toe with the right thumb and fingers
- Raise the left arm from front to shoulder level
- Stay in the position breathing normally
- Exhale, bring the right leg down to the floor, and the arms down to the sides
- Repeat on the other side

For advanced practitioners:

- Bend the right knee and lift the leg up
- Inhale, raise the right leg up and back, turning the shoulder and right elbow to bring the right arm behind the head
- Elbow should be pointing up, with the right foot near the back of the head
- Raise the left arm from front to shoulder level
- Stay in the position breathing normally
- Exhale, bring the right leg down to the floor, and the arms down to the sides
- Repeat on the other side

III-21 Natrajāsana: Lord of Dance Posture (cont.)

⚠ **Caution:**

People with vertigo, cardiac problems, spinal disorders, weak knee joints etc should avoid this posture.

✓ **Effects & Benefits:**

This Āsana tones and strengthens the legs, chest, shoulder and back muscles. It Improves balance and concentration.

III-22 Uthita Hasta Pādaṅguṣṭāsana: Raised hand to big toe posture

Instructions:

- Stand in Samasthithi
- Fix the gaze on a fixed point in front
- Lift the right knee and thigh close to the chest
- Hold the right big toe with the thumb, index and middle fingers of the right hand
- Inhale and slowly straighten the right leg
- Stay in the posture with breathing normally
- Exhale and bring the right leg down, bringing the arm down to the sides
- Repeat on the other side

⚠ Caution:

People with hip, knee joint disorders, sciatica etc may avoid this posture.

✓ Effects & Benefits:

This Āsana improves neuromuscular coordination. Hip and leg muscles are toned and strengthened.

III-23 Adhomukha Śvānāsana: Downward facing Dog

Instructions:

- Stand in Samasthithi
- Inhale and raise the arms from the front
- Exhale and bend forward from the hips to place hands besides the feet
- The legs should be straight, with the arms and shoulder relaxed, and forehead should touch the knees
- Hold and take both the legs back, shifting the weight to the hands
- Keep the body in a horizontal position balancing on toes and hands, while the knees, abdomen and chest are off the floor
- Keep the feet together, while the elbows are bent and chin is down
- Inhale and bring the chest forward, straightening the arms and elbows
- The whole body is balanced on hands and toes
- Exhale and lift the hips up, bringing the head and chest down
- The legs should be straight, the feet on the floor and the crown of the head should touch the floor
- Stay in the position breathing normally
- Hold and bring the legs forward, placing feet between hands
- Inhale and raise the arms from the front and come up
- Exhale and bring the arms down to the sides

⚠ **Caution:**

People with high blood pressure, heart ailments, weak shoulders and arms, retinal problems etc. should avoid this posture.

✓ **Effects & Benefits:**

This Āsana strengthens arms and legs, stretches hamstrings and shoulders, and energises the body.

III-24 Garudāsana: The Eagle Posture

Instructions:

- Stand in Samasthithi
- Focus the gaze on a fixed point in front
- Bend the right knee
- Take the left leg over the right thigh above right knee
- Bring the left foot behind right calf and lock left big toe at inner side of right ankle
- Keep the arms at chest level and bend the elbows
- Intertwine the forearms with the left elbow supporting the right
- Clasp the palms together
- Stay in the position taking three to five breaths
- Repeat on the other side, with the left leg entwining the right leg and the left arm entwining the right arm
- Releasing the legs and arms, come back to Samasthiti

⚠ **Caution:**

People with knee and ankle joint disorders, balancing issues etc may practice with caution or avoid this posture.

✓ **Effects & Benefits:**

This Āsana improves neuromuscular coordination. Muscles of arms & legs are strengthened.

III-25 Uttanā Prṣtāsana: Lizard Posture

Instructions:

- Exhale and come to Adhomukhaswanāsana, the palms and feet firmly fixed on the ground
- Inhale and take the right foot forward to place it outside the right hand
- Keep the forearms on the floor and interlock the fingers
- The right knee should be bent and the right foot firmly on the floor
- The left leg should be straight and supported on toes
- The head and spine should be straight
- Hold the position breathing normally
- Exhale and bring the right foot back to Adomukhasvanāsana
- Repeat on the other side

⚠ **Caution:**

People with weak joints, back pain, pelvic disorders etc. should avoid this posture.

✓ **Effects & Benefits:**

This Āsana improves hips and groin flexibility, strengthens hamstrings, quadriceps and leg muscles. It tones and strengthens arms and shoulder muscles.

(Yoga Sutra 2.32)

sauca-santosa-tapah-svâdhyâyesvara-prañidhânâni niyamâh

Internal and external purification of the body and mind, developing an attitude of contentment, discipline, self-study and reflection on sacred words along with an attitude of surrender are the observances or practices of self-training also called as Niyamās, the second rung or limb of Yoga. Practicing the observances mentioned above - ensures that we take care of ourselves mentally and physically. Self-care and self-love are equally important, along with a healthy life to guide us to higher states of awareness.

IV Kneeling Āsanas

V-26 Vajrāsana (Diamond posture)

Instructions:
Vajra in Sanskrit means diamond, so this is called diamond posture

- Sit in Daṇḍāsana
- Bend the legs at knees to sit on the heels
- Keep the spine erect, hands resting on the knees
- Place the right big toe over the left one
- Stay in the position breathing normally

Note: This is the only posture which can be done after meals to aid digestion. This posture is the base position for kneeling postures.

⚠ Caution:
People with knee problems should avoid this posture.

✓ Effects & Benefits:
This Āsana helps in relieving constipation and helps digestion. It stretches the quadriceps muscles and prepares the lower body for meditative postures.

IV-27 Śaśāṅkāsana: Hare Posture

Instructions:

- Sit in Vajrāāsana with the spine erect and the head straight
- Inhale, raise the arms from the front
- Exhale, and bend forward bending from the hips to place the palms on the floor
- Keep the arms straight with theforehead touching the floor
- Stay in the position breathing normally
- Inhale, raise the arms up and come up
- Exhale, bring the arms down to starting position

⚠ Caution:

People with spinal disorders, vertigo, and hypertension should practice with caution or avoid the posture.

✓ Effects & Benefits:

This Āsana strengthens back, pelvic muscles and helps to prevent constipation.

IV-28 Mārjārāsana: Cat Posture

Instructions:

- Sit in Vajrāāsana with the spine erect and the head straight
- Inhale, raise the arms from the front
- Exhale, bend forward from the hips to place the palms on the floor
- Keep the arms straight, forehead touching the floorPress the palms on the floor to move forward, and bring the thighs perpendicular to the floor; hands should be in line with the knees
- Inhale and lift the head up, arching the back to make it concave
- Exhale and contract the abdomen bringing head down making the back convex
- Stay in the position breathing normally
- Inhale, come up raising the arms from the front
- Exhale and come back to starting position

⚠ Caution:

People with spinal disorders, knee pain and cervical issues may practice with caution or avoid this posture.

✓ Effects & Benefits:

This Āsana improves flexibility of spine, neck and shoulders. Helps in prevention of back pain and menstrual disorders.

IV– 29 Vyāghrāsana: Tiger Posture

Instructions:

- Sit in Vajrāāsana
- Inhale, raise the arms from the front
- Exhale, bend forward from the hips to place palms on the floor
- Keep arms straight, forehead touching the floor
- Inhale and move forward, lifting the head up arching the back simultaneously stretching the right leg up
- Bend the right knee and look up, bringing the right foot towards the back of the head
- Stay in the position for a few seconds, breathing normally
- Exhale and straighten the right leg, bending head down to bring the right knee towards the nose
- Stay in the position for a few seconds breathing normally
- Inhale and straighten the leg arching the back, head up
- Exhale and stretch back bringing the head down and the forehead touching the floor
- Repeat with the left leg

⚠ **Caution:**

People with knee pain, back pain, hernia should avoid this posture.

✓ **Effects & Benefits:**

This Āsana strengthens back and neck muscles and improves spinal flexibility.

(Yoga Sutra 2.46)

sthira-sukham âsanam

The means of perfecting a posture is that of relaxing, relenting effort, and allowing your attention to merge with endlessness, or the infinite. As soon as we start practicing a yoga posture, we find all sorts of disturbances in our body; but with regular practice we come to a stage where we slowly lose the sense of body consciousness, where we feel neither pain nor pleasure. Only when we reach this state with our physical body can our mind be rested. By slowly reaching a state unaffected by the disturbances of the mind, we can finally think of the infinite which exists beyond the body and the mind.

Āsana is not just the physical posture practice most people envision when they think of yoga. It is not about being as flexible as the person next to you, but about seeing what your body can do, and using the physical practice as an expression of steadiness and ease and to go beyond the impermanence of the body and mind.

V Seated Āsanas

V-30 Daṇḍāsana (Staff posture)

Instructions:

- Sit on the floor with your legs stretched forward
- Keep the thighs, knees, ankles and feet together
- Place the palms on the floor, or on the knees
- The back, neck and head should be straight.
- Shoulders should be relaxed
- Close the eyes and relax the whole body in this position
- Daṇḍāsana is the (Samasthithi) starting position for all seated postures

⚠ **Caution:**

People with knee problems, spine issues, and lower back pain may avoid sitting on floor.

✓ **Effects & Benefits:**

Regular practise of this Āsana improves posture.

V-31 Jānu Sīrṣāsana (Head to knee posture)

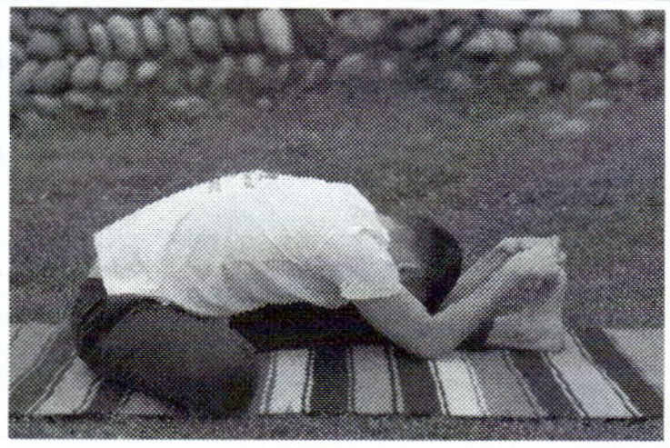

Instructions:

- Sit in Daṇḍāsana (seated Samasthithi)
- Bend the left leg at the knee to place the sole of the left foot to touch the right inner thigh near the groin
- Inhale, raise the arms up stretching the upper torso
- Exhale, bend forward from the hips stretching the back to touch the forehead to the knee bringing hands down to hold the right heel/ toe
- Keep the right leg and back relaxed
- Stay in the position breathing normally
- Inhale and come up slowly raising arms up
- Exhale and bring arms down to the sides to sit back in Daṇḍāsana
- Repeat on the other side

⚠ **Caution:**

People with dizziness, lower back pain, slipped disc, and pregnant women should avoid the posture.

✓ **Effects & Benefits:**

This Āsana stretches the spine, strengthens shoulders, calves and leg muscles. It Helps in improving digestion and tones abdominal muscles and organs.

V-32 Paśchimōthānāsana (Back stretching posture)

Instructions:

- Sit in Daṇḍāsana (seated samasthithi).
- Inhale, raise arms from the front stretching the upper torso
- Exhale, bend forward from the hips stretching the back to touch the forehead to the knees bringing hands down to encircle the toes
- Keep the back and legs relaxed, elbows on the floor and deepen the forward bend
- Stay in the position breathing normally
- Inhale and slowly come up raising the arms up from the front
- Exhale and bring arms down to the sides to sit in Daṇḍāsana

⚠ **Caution:**

People with dizziness, lower back pain, slipped disc, and pregnant women should avoid the posture.

✓ **Effects & Benefits:**

Stretches and strengthens the spine, shoulders, calves and leg muscles. It helps in improving digestion, tones and strengthens abdominal muscles and organs.

V-33 Ardhapadmāsana (Half-Lotus Posture)

Instructions:

- Sit in Daṇḍāsana
- Relax the shoulders, keep the chin down and youreyes closed
- Bend the left leg and tuck the left foot under the right foreleg
- Place the right foot on top of the left thigh near the left hip
- Keep the spine, neck and head straight, and place your palms on the knees
- Stay in the position breathing normally relaxing the whole body

⚠ **Caution:**

People with knee, and spinal problems should not practice this posture.

✓ **Effects & Benefits:**

This Āsana removes tension in the inner thigh muscles, removes tiredness from long hours of standing and walking and calms the mind.

V- 34 Padmāsana (Lotus Posture)

Instructions:

- Sit in Daṇḍāsana
- Relax the shoulders, keep the chin down and youreyes closed
- Bend the right leg at the knee and place the right foot on top of the left thigh near the hip
- Place the left foot on top of the right thigh near the hip
- The soles of the feet should face upwards
- Keep the spine, neck and head straight, your chin down and let the palms rest on the knees
- Stay in the position breathing normally

⚠ Caution:

People with ankles, knees and back problems should practice with caution or avoid this posture.

✓ Effects & Benefits:

This Āsana calms the mind and relaxes the body. It helps to steady the body and mind to be still while meditating.

V-35 Sukhāsana (Easy seated posture)

Instructions:

- Sit in Daṇḍāsana
- Fold the legs at the knees and bring the heels of the feet under the opposite legs
- Keep the spine erect, the head and neck straight with hands resting on the knees
- Stay in the position breathing normally

⚠ **Caution:**

Avoid the posture in case of leg or knee problems.

✓ **Effects & Benefits:**

This Āsana strengthens the muscles of ankles, knees and hip joints and prepares the body for meditative postures.

V-36 Yogāsana (Forward bending in Lotus Position)

Instructions:

- Sit in the Padmāsana/Ardha padmāsana or sukhāsana
- Inhale, raise both the arms from the front
- Exhale and sweep the arms back, simultaneously bending from the hips to bring the arms downs, palms on the floor
- Spine should be straight, touching the forehead on the floor and the body should be relaxed
- Stay in the position breathing three to five breaths
- Inhale and slowly come up bringing the arms up
- Exhale and bring the arms down to the sides

⚠ **Caution:**

People with asthma, spinal disorders, knee pain, digestive issues, and ulcers should avoid this posture.

✓ **Effects & Benefits:**

This Āsana stretches and strengthens the arms and spine. It tones and strengthens the abdominal muscles and organs.

V-37 Kākāsana (Crow posture)

Instructions:

- Stand with your feet apart with the hands by the sides
- Inhale and raise the arms from the front to shoulder level
- Exhale and squat down with the buttocks touching the ankles
- Place your hands on the knees
- Stay in the position breathing normally
- Inhale and come up with the arms extended forward to shoulder level
- Exhale and bring the arms down to the sides

⚠ Caution:

People with knee and back problems should avoid the posture.

Effects & Benefits:

Strengthens hamstrings and quadriceps. It massages and tones abdominal organs, and improves digestion.

V-38 Kākacalanam (Crow walk)

Instructions:

- Stand with the feet shoulder width apart, the arms by the sides
- Inhale, raise the arms from the front to shoulder level
- Exhale, squat down with the buttocks touching the ankles
- Take small steps on your toes in the squatting position
- When one step is taken forward, bring the opposite knee to the floor
- Keep walking, taking fifteen to twenty steps or more, breathing normally
- Inhale and come up with the arms extended forward to shoulder level
- Exhale and bring the arms down to the sides

⚠ Caution:

People with knee and back problems should avoid this posture.

✓ Effects & Benefits:

This Āsana strengthens hamstrings and quadriceps. It massages and tones the abdominal organs, improves digestion.

V-39 Vakrāsana (Half Spinal Twist)

Instructions:

- Sit in Daṇḍāsana
- Keep the spine straight, bend the right leg at the knee and bring it close to the chest
- Place the right foot outside the left knee with the sole of the right foot resting on the floor
- The left leg should be straight on the floor
- Inhale, raise the arms from the front
- Exhale, place the right arm behind the body with fingers pointing out and take the left arm over the right knee to clasp the right ankle
- Twist the torso to the right, turning the head to the right to look over the right shoulder
- Stay in the position breathing normally
- Inhale and release the posture by gently turning the head to the centre and bring the arms up
- Exhale and bring the arms down to the sides
- Repeat on the other side

⚠ **Caution:**

People with neck/cervical, hips and back problems should avoid this posture.

✓ **Effects & Benefits:**

This Āsana helps to make the spine flexible. It massages and tones abdominal organs and helps to remove belly fat. It improves digestion and increases blood circulation in the pelvic region.

V-40 Ardhamatsyendrāsana (Half) Sage Matsyendra posture

Instructions:

- Sit in Daṇḍāsana
- Keeping the spine straight, bend the left leg and place the left leg under the right thigh with the sole of the foot close to the right buttock
- Bend the right leg at the knee and place the right foot outside the left knee
- Right knee should be straight and the left knee on the floor
- Inhale and raise the arms up
- Exhale and twist to the right bringing the left hand to hold the right ankle by gently pushing the right knee with left elbow
- Take the right arm to encircle the back to place the right palm on the left thigh
- Turn the head to the right to look over the right shoulder
- Stay in the position breathing normally
- Inhale and release the posture by gently turning the head to the centre, releasing the right arm from the left thigh and the left arm from the right ankle and bring the arms down
- Exhale,stretch the legs and relax
- Repeat on the other side

⚠ **Caution:**

People with neck/cervical, hips and knee problems should avoid this posture.

✓ **Effects & Benefits:**

This Āsana helps to make the spine, shoulder and neck more flexible. It massages the abdominal organs, removes belly fat, improves digestion and increases blood circulation in the pelvic region.

V-41 Gomukhāsana (Cow face posture)

Instructions:

- Sit in Daṇḍāsana
- Keeping the spine straight, bend the left leg and place the left leg under the thigh with the sole of the foot close to the right buttock
- Bend the right leg at the knee so that the right leg crosses over the left leg from the top with the right knee over the left (to resemble mouth of a cow) and right foot brought alongside the left buttock (both the feet on either side to resemble ears of a cow). Hands are by the sides in front with fingers touching the floor.
- Inhale and raise the right arm above the head and bend it at the elbow to place the back of the palm behind the left shoulder.
- Exhale taking the left arm behind the back with elbow pointing down. The back of the palm should touch the back to gently grip the fingers of the right hand coming from above.
- Stay in the position breathing normally.
- Keep the awareness on the expansion in the chest and the stretch in the arms.
- Exhale and stretch legs and relax
- Repeat on the other side

⚠ **Caution:**

People with neck issues, shoulder pain and tight hips may avoid this posture.

✓ **Effects & Benefits:**

This Āsana helps to strengthen the respiratory system increasing lung capacity. It helps to tone arms, removes shoulder stiffness and strengthens back muscles.

V-42 Maṇḍukāsana (Frog Posture)

Instructions:
- Sit in Vajrāsana
- Inhale, making fists of both the hands with thumbs inside the fingers
- Place the fists on either side of the navel
- Exhale and bend forward, pressing the navel with fists to place the chin down and look straight
- Stay in the position breathing normally
- Inhale and slowly come up
- Exhale, release the fists to place the hands on the thighs and relax

Note: In this posture, the knees can be kept close to each other or spread apart, as two acceptable variations.

⚠ **Caution:**
People with weak knees, hernia, or abdominal injuries should avoid this posture.

✓ **Effects & Benefits:**
This Āsana helps to massage the abdominal organs, tones abdominal muscles and helps to improve the digestive system. It strengthens the back muscles and spine.

V-43 Uthana Maṇdukāsana (Extended Frog Posture)

Instructions:

- Sit in Vajrāsana
- Spread the knees wide apart keeping toes together
- Inhale, raise the arms from the front with palms facing up
- Exhale, and cross the arms behind the head to place the hands on the upper back on opposite shoulders
- Keep the back and neck straight
- Stay in the posture breathing normally
- Inhale, and raise the arms up from the front
- Exhale and bring the hands down to the sides
- Relax in Vajrāsana

⚠ **Caution:**

People with weak knees, back problems, and hip pain should avoid this posture.

✓ **Effects & Benefits:**

This Āsana stretches and strengthens shoulder blades and upper arms. It strengthens the respiratory system increasing lung capacity. It increases blood circulation and tones abdominal muscles.

V-44 Simhāsana (Lion Posture)

Instructions:

- Sit in Vajrāsana.
- Spread the knees wide apart, keeping toes together
- Move the body slightly forward to place the hands on the floor in front between the knees, fingers pointing inwards
- Arms should be straight andthe back arched
- Tilt the head back, open the mouth wide and extend the tongue out towards the chin
- Inhale slowly in this position
- Exhale and bring the eyes to focus on the centre of the eyebrows
- Inhale through the nose
- Exhale and make a continuous roaring 'Haaa' sound coming from deep within the throat
- Stay in the position keeping the awareness on the throat
- Inhale through the nose, closing the mouth
- Repeat the cycle a few times
- Relax in Vajrāsana

⚠ **Caution:**

People having dizziness or vertigo need can avoid focus on the centre of the eyebrows. The "Haaa" sound should not be too loud. It should be deep and steady.

✓ **Effects & Benefits:**

This Āsana helps to open up the throat and exercises facial muscles. It is very helpful for people who stammer. It energises and activates the throat centre.

V-45 Ardha Uṣtrāsana (Half Camel Posture)

Instructions:

- Sit in Vajrāsana
- Keep the feet and knees shoulder width apart
- Come up on the knees with the torso perpendicular to the ground,hands by the sides
- Inhale, raise the right arm up slowly in a circulatory movement above the head arching the back
- Exhale, bring the hips forward, arching the back to bring the right arm down to clasp the right ankle
- Simultaneously raise the left arm above the head in a vertical position, stretching the neck to drop the head back
- Move the head back as far comfortable. Do not strain. Both shoulders should be aligned
- Stay in the position breathing normally
- Inhale and come up to kneeling position bringing the arms up
- Exhale and bring the arms down to the sides to sit in Vajrāsana
- Repeat on the other side

⚠ **Caution:**

People with cervical problems, vertigo, back, neck, shoulder or knee pain should avoid this posture.

✓ **Effects & Benefits:**

This Āsana stretches and opens up the chest, stimulates the respiratory, digestive and endocrine system.

V-46 Uṣṭrāsana (Camel Posture)

Instructions:

- Sit in Vajrāsana
- Inhale, raise the arms from the front to come up on the knees with the torso perpendicular to the ground
- Exhale, lower the arms from the front to place hands on the lower back with bent elbows
- Inhale and arch the back, moving the hands down to clasp the heels
- Stretch the neck and drop the head back
- Move the head as far back as comfortable. Do not strain your neck
- Stay in the position breathing normally
- Inhale and come up to kneeling position bringing the arms up
- Exhale and bring the arms down to the sides to sit in Vajrāsana

⚠ **Caution:**
People with cervical issues, vertigo, back, neck, shoulder and knee problems should avoid this posture.

✓ **Effects & Benefits:**
This Āsana stretches and opens up the chest, stimulates the respiratory, digestive and endocrine systems.

V-47 Bhūnamanāsana (Spinal Twist Prostration posture)

Instructions:

- Sit in Daṇḍāsana
- Inhale, raise the arms up from the front
- Exhale and twist to the right side, bringing the arms down to place the right hand behind and left hand near the right hip, touching the forehead to the floor
- Stay in the position breathing normally
- Inhale and come up raising the arms up
- Exhale and bring the arms down to the sides
- Repeat on the other side

⚠ **Caution:**

People with spinal problems, weak wrists, and hernia may avoid this posture.

✓ **Effects & Benefits:**

This Āsana increases the flexibility of the spine, stretches and strengthens the lower back.

V-48 Upviṣṭakōṇāsana: Seated Angle posture

Instructions:

- Sit in Daṇḍāsana
- Spread the legs wide apart, place pams on the floor
- Inhale, raise arms up from the front, with the palms facing up
- Exhale, bend forward from the hips to place the palms and elbows on the floor
- Touch the forehead to the floor, keeping the arms straight and relaxed
- Stay in the position breathing normally
- Inhale, raise the arms and come up
- Exhale, lower the arms to the sides and relax

⚠ **Caution:**

People with knee, hip disorders, back pain etc should avoid this posture.

✓ **Effects & Benefits:**

This Āsana strengthens hamstring muscles and is beneficial for the pelvic region and prevents menstrual disorders. It brings flexibility to the lower back, tones and strengthens the abdomen.

V-49 Baddhakōṇāsana: Bound angle Posture

Instructions:

- Sit in Daṇḍāsana
- Exhale, bend the knees to bring heels near the pelvis, soles of the feet pressed together
- Hold the arch of the foot with both hands
- Keep the back straight, the heels touching the groin, the chin parallel to floor and shoulders relaxed
- Stay in the position breathing normally
- Inhale, release the hands, stretch the legs forward and relax in the starting position

⚠ **Caution:**

People with knee, ankle joint, hip disorders, back pain etc may avoid this posture.

✓ **Effects & Benefits:**

This Āsana strengthens hamstring muscles, is beneficial for the pelvic region, and prevents menstrual disorders.

V-50 Catuṣpāda Pitham: Four Legs Posture

Instructions:

- Sit in Daṇḍāsana
- Exhale, bend the knees, keep the feet on the ground, the knees together and thefeet together
- Place the palms on the mat behind the back with fingers pointing forward
- Inhale and raise the trunk up, with the body weight evenly supported by palms and feet
- Drop the head back
- Keep the feet vertical, and perpendicular to the thighs
- Keep the arms and legs in line at shoulder width
- Stay in the position breathing normally
- Exhale and lower the trunk to the floor, the knees bent and thefeet together, with the palms on the floor
- Inhale and stretch the legs and relax in the starting position

⚠ **Caution:**
People with shoulder, neck, knee/ankle joint or hip disorders should avoid this posture.

✓ **Effects & Benefits:**
This Āsana strengthens leg muscles, shoulders, wrists, thighs and abdominal organs.

V-51 Pūrvatanāsana: East facing intense stretch

Instructions:

- Sit in Daṇḍāsana
- Place the hands on the mat behind the back, and your fingers pointing forward
- Inhale and raise the trunk up, body weight supported evenly between arms and legs
- Drop the head back
- Keep the legs and arms straight, with the feet together on the floor
- Stay in the position breathing normally
- Exhale and bring the trunk to the floor, the legs extended forward and relax in the starting position

⚠ **Caution:**

People with shoulder, arms, wrists, knee, ankle joints, and hip disorders should avoid this posture.

✓ **Effects & Benefits:**

This Āsana strengthens leg muscles, shoulders, wrists and abdominal organs.

V-52 Ardha Kapotāsana Preparatory: Half Pigeon posture

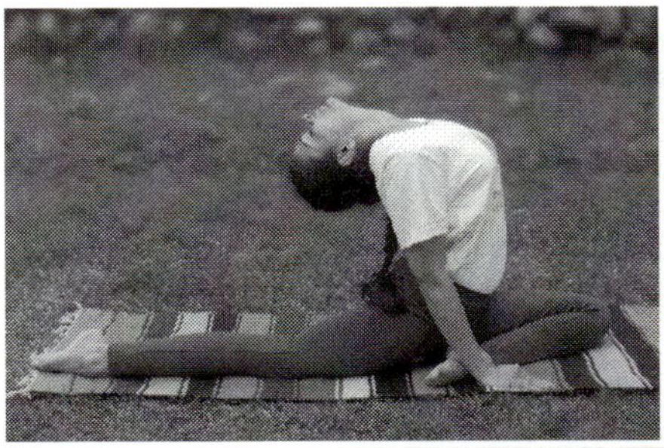

Instructions:

- Sit in Daṇḍāsana
- Place the right leg on the floor, the rightknee bent with the right heel towards the perineum
- Keep the left leg in Vajrāsana position
- Rotate the left leg and bend the leg at the knee
- Raise both arms arching the back and clasp the left foot with both hands above the head
- Maintain the position breathing normally
- For releasing the posture, release the arms and the left foot. Simultaneously, bring the left leg back to the floor and relax the back
- Rotate the left leg back to original position and straighten the right leg
- Relax the legs in daṇḍāsana
- Repeat for the other side

⚠ Caution:

People with disorders at pelvic, shoulder, knee and ankle joints should avoid doing this posture.

✓ Effects & Benefits:

This Āsana strengthens legs and arm muscles. It improves functioning of abdominal and thoracic organs.

V-53 Kapotāsana: Pigeon Posture

Instructions:

- Adopt Ushtrāsana standing on the knees bending backwards
- Push the lower part of the trunk up and the tailbone downwards
- Head on the feet elbows on floor near ears and palms at crown of the head
- Stay in the position breathing normally
- Release the posture, move the hands to lift the head up and with support of elbows slowly come up

Note: This is an advanced āsana, to be practised only after sufficient flexibility is attained.

⚠ **Caution:**

People with spine, shoulder, knees, ankle joints, hip disorders, hernia etc. should avoid this posture.

✓ **Effects & Benefits:**

This Āsana strengthens the spine, leg muscles, hips, shoulders, wrists, abdominal organs and chest.

V-54 Supta Vajrāsana: Lying Diamond Posture

Instructions:

- Sit in Vajrāsana, knees together, with the heels pointing outward and the big toes touching
- Keep the spine erect and the hands should be resting on your thighs
- Place the hands on the floor behind the back, bend the elbows and lean back slowly to place the elbows on the ground
- Inhale and lower the back of the head to the ground, arching the back
- Rest the hands on the thighs. Or raise your hands above your head and place them under the head after crossing them so that the right palm is below the left shoulder and the left palm is below the right shoulder
- Stay in the position, breathing normally
- Exhale and come back to the starting position, with the support of your elbows and arms

⚠ Caution:

People suffering from neck problems, knee problems, stiff ankles, back pain and sciatica, should avoid this posture.

✓ Effects & Benefits:

This Āsana stimulates and strengthens the abdominal organs to function effectively, helps in digestive problems. It strengthens the spine, good for the thyroid gland, and expands the chest. It is beneficial for people suffering from Asthma, and lung related conditions.

V-55 Navāsana: Boat posture

Instructions:

- Sit with the legs together and stretched forward, keeping the feet together, the back straight and the palms on the knees, toes facing up
- Inhale, raise the arms up from the front, with the palms facing up
- Exhale, bring the arms down to shoulder level, with palms facing down and simultaneously lifting legs up straight. Maintain the balance on the hips, keeping the palms besides raised legs
- Stay in the position breathing normally
- Inhale, raise the arms up and lower the legs to the floor
- Exhale and lower the arms to the sides, and shift back to starting position

⚠ **Caution:**

People with weak digestion, back pain, hip, knee, or neck injury, menstruating or pregnant women should avoid this posture.

✓ **Effects & Benefits:**

This Āsana helps in strengthening the abdomen, spine, hip flexors and improves digestion. It stimulates the thyroid gland, kidneys, prostate glands and intestines helping them to function effectively. This Āsana helps in developing physical and mental balance.

V-56 Bālāsana: Child Posture

Instructions:

- Sit in Vajrāsana with the spine erect, keeping thehead straight
- Move the thighs apart
- Inhale, raise the arms up from the front
- Exhale, bring the trunk forward between thighs
- Bring the arms down, touch the forehead and palms on the floor
- Stay in the position breathing normally
- Inhale and raise the arms up
- Exhale and bring the arms down
- Relax in the starting position

⚠ **Caution:**

People with knee and ankle joint disorders may avoid this posture.

✓ **Effects & Benefits:**

This Āsana helps in reducing stress and fatigue. Improves flexibility of ankle, knee, spine and shoulders.

(Yoga Sutra 2.49)

tasmin sati svâsa-prasvâsayor gati-vicchedah prâñâyâmah

Once a posture has been achieved or conquered, you will begin to incorporate breath control, or prānāyāma. Controlling the motion of the exhalation and the inhalation is the fourth of the eight limbs or rungs. Prāna is not the breath, though the word is loosely used for breath, it is the sum total of the cosmic energy. The manifestation of prāna in the body is the motion of the lungs. Drawing in of the breath is caused by prāna and regulation of breath is the easiest way to regulate and control the prāna or the vital force.

Prānāyāma is an important aspect of the āsana practice and should be utilized during your time on the mat. Without the breath, the physical practice is incomplete and can become disconnected from your mental focus and control.

VI Supine Postures

VI-57 Śavāsana: Corpse Posture

Instructions:

- Lie down on the back
- Keep the feet slightly apart and relaxed
- Place the arms slightly away from the sides of the body, with the palms facing up and relaxed
- With eyes closed, relax the whole body
- Breathing should be normal and relaxed

Effects & Benefits:

This Āsana relaxes the whole body and mind, relieves fatigue, stress, and very beneficial for people with high blood pressure.

VI-58 Pavanamuktāsana: Wind Relieving Posture

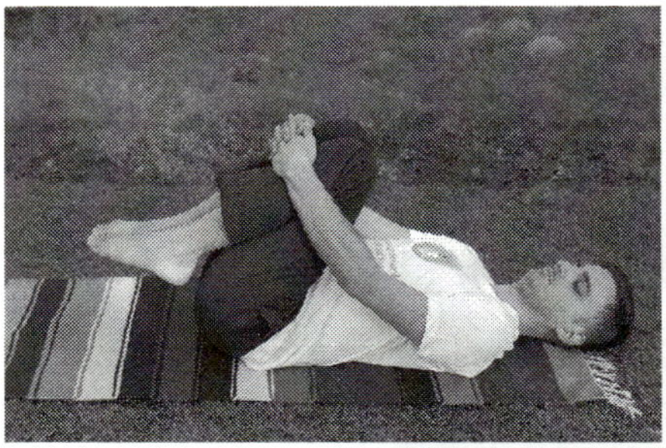

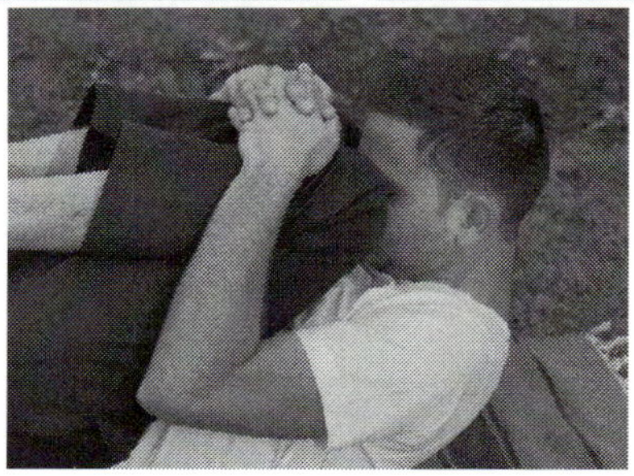

Instructions:

- Lie down on the back, keeping the legs together and straight, the feet together, and the arms by the side of the body
- Bend the knees, placingthe feet on the ground close to the body
- Clasp the knees with both hands and lift the feet off the floor
- Inhale in that position
- Exhale, bring the knees towards the chest, simultaneously lifting the head and shoulders to bring the forehead to touch the knees
- Stay in the position breathing normally
- Inhale and slowly bring the head, shoulders and feet down to the ground

⚠ **Caution:**

People with high blood pressure, sciatica, slipped disc, hernia, and cervical issues should avoid this posture.

✓ **Effects & Benefits:**

This Āsana strengthens the back, tones the abdomen, stimulates the digestive system, helps to relieve gas, acidity, and constipation.

VI-59 Ardha Pavanamuktāsana: Half Wind Relieving Posture

Instructions:
- Lie down on the back, keeping the legs together and straight, the feet together, and the arms by the side of the body
- Inhale, bend the right knee and clasp the knee with both hands to bring it close to the chest
- The left leg should be straight on the ground
- Exhale, raise the head and shoulders off the floor and bring forehead to touch the right knee
- Stay in the position breathing normally
- Inhale and bring the head and shoulders back to the floor
- Exhale and come back to the starting position, bringing the right leg to the floor and the arms by the sides of the body
- Repeat the same with the left leg

⚠ **Caution:**
People with cervical problems, high blood pressure, hernia, slipped disc, and sciatica should avoid this posture.

✓ **Effects & Benefits:**
This Āsana strengthens the back, stimulates the digestive organs and helps in relieving digestive problems like gas, bloating, acidity and constipation.

VI-60 Sethubandhāsana: Bridge Posture

Instructions:

- Lie down on the back, keeping the feet together, the arms by the sides, and the chin down
- Bend the legs at the knees and place the feet on the floor close to the buttocks, keeping the knees together and the feet together
- Inhale, lifting the hips off the floor
- Stay in the position breathing normally
- Exhale and bring the hips down to the floor
- Stretch the legs and relax

⚠ **Caution:**
People with acid reflux, neck or back injury should avoid this posture.

✓ **Effects & Benefits:**
This Āsana helps to strengthen the back and knees, stimulates the thyroid gland, and opens up the chest.

VI-61 Naukāsana: Boat Posture

Instructions:

- Lie on the back keeping the legs together, the feet together and the hands by the sides.
- Inhale in that position.
- Exhale, raise the legs, the arms, the head and chest off the floor
- The arms and toes should be in the same level, with the palms facing down
- Stay in the position breathing normally, focussing on the toes
- Exhale and come back to the starting position and relax

⚠ **Caution:**

People with low blood pressure, cervical problems, and migraines should avoid this posture. Women should avoid this posture during pregnancy and menstruation.

✓ **Effects & Benefits:**

This Āsana works on all the organs in the abdominal area to function effectively. It stimulates the digestive and nervous system.

VI-62 Ūrdhva Prasrta Pādāsana: Upward Extension Leg Posture

Instructions:

- Lie down on the back, legs together and straight, feet together, arms by the sides, palms on the floor and thechin down
- Inhale, raise the arms from the front to place them on the floor above the head
- Arms should be straight with the palms turned up.
- Exhale, raise both the legs up keeping them straight while bringing arms down to the sides
- Stay in the position breathing normally
- Inhale, raise the arms up above the head to place them on the floor simultaneously lowering the legs down
- Exhale and bring the arms down to the sides

⚠ **Caution:**

People with neck pain, lower back pain and sciatica should avoid this posture.

✓ **Effects & Benefits:**

This Āsana tones and strengthens abdominal muscles. It tones and strengthens the abdominal muscles and reduces belly fat. It Improves digestion and helps to reduce gastric problems.

VI-63 Supta Eka Padāṅguṣṭāsana: Lying Big Toe Posture

Instructions:

- Lie down on the back, the legs straight, feet together, palms on the floor, the arms along the sides of the body and chin down
- Inhale, raise the arms from the front to place them on the floor above the head
- Arms should be straight with the palms turned up
- Exhale, lift the right leg up, simultaneously bringing the right arm to hold the big toe with the right thumb and fingers
- Left leg should be straight on the floor and the left arm by the side of the body
- Stay in the position breathing normally
- Inhale, release the hold on the big toe bringing the right leg down to the floor and the right arm on the floor above the head
- Exhale and bring the right arm down to the sides, palms facing down
- Repeat on the other side

⚠ **Caution:**

People with injury to hamstrings or quadriceps, tight shoulders, and cervical issues should avoid the posture.

✓ **Effects & Benefits:**

This Āsana relieves stiffness in the lower back, strengthens legs and knee joints, stimulates and strengthens all the abdominal muscles and organs.

VI-64 Supta Padāṅguṣṭāsana: Lying Big Toes Posture

Instructions:

- Lie down on the back, legs together and straight, feet together, arms by the sides, palms on the floor and the chin down
- Inhale, raise the arms from the front to place them on the floor above the head
- Arms should be straight with the palms turned up
- Exhale, lift both the legs up straight, and simultaneously bring the arms down to hold the big toes with respective thumbs and fingers.
- Hips should be on the floor, the neck and shoulders relaxed and the chin down
- Stay in the position breathing normally
- Inhale and release the toes and lower the legs down to the floor, bringing the arms to the floor above the head
- Exhale and bring the arms down to the floor along the sides of the body, with the palms facing down

⚠ **Caution:**

People with injury to hamstrings or quadriceps, tight shoulders and cervical issues should avoid this posture.

✓ **Effects & Benefits:**

This Āsana gives a good stretch to the legs, hips, and hamstrings. Strengthens the abdominal muscles, knee joints, stimulates the digestive organs and improves digestion.

VI-65 Supta Prasārita Padāṅguṣṭāsana: Lying Spreading Legs Big Toe Posture

Instructions:

- Lie down on the back, legs together and straight, feet together, arms by the sides, palms on the floor and the chin down
- Inhale, raise the arms from the front to place them on the floor above the head
- Arms should be straight with the palms turned up
- Exhale, lift both legs up straight, simultaneously bringing the arms down to hold the big toes with respective thumbs and fingers
- Hips should be on the floor, the neck and shoulders relaxed and thechin down
- Inhale and open the legs sideways
- Stay in the position breathing normally
- Exhale and bring the legs together and come to Supta Padangusthāsana
- Inhale, release the toes and bring the legs down to the floor straight, bringing the arms to the floor above the head
- Exhale and bring the arms down to the floor along the side of the body, with the palms facing down

⚠ **Caution:**

People with injury to hamstrings or quadriceps, tight shoulders and cervical issues should avoid this posture.

✓ **Effects & Benefits:**

This Āsana gives a good stretch to the legs, hips, and hamstrings. Strengthens the abdominal muscles, hip joints, knee joints, stimulates the digestive organs, and improves digestion.

VI-66 Supta Baddha Kōṇāsana: Lying Bound Angle Posture

Instructions:

- Lie down on the back, legs together and straight, feet together, arms by the sides, palms on the floor and the chin down
- Exhale, bend the knees to place the feet close to the buttocks, keeping knees together and the feet together
- Open the knees and place them on the floor bringing the soles of the feet against each other
- Place the hands on the abdomen locking fingers and turning them out
- Inhale and raise the arms, placing them on the floor above the head
- Maintain the posture breathing normally
- Exhale and lower the arms down, unlocking the fingers and bringing the knees together
- Inhale and straighten the legs back to starting position, arms by the sides

⚠ **Caution:**

People having neck, spine, hip, or knee injury, low back pain, or sciatica should avoid the posture.

✓ **Effects & Benefits:**

This Āsana stretches the groin and inner thighs, stimulates the abdominal organs, the ovaries, kidneys, prostate gland, and bladder to function effectively.

VI-67 Skandharāsana: Shoulder Posture

Instructions:

- Lie down on the back, legs together and straight, feet together, arms by the sides, palms on the floor and the chin down
- Bend the knees, bringing the feet closer to the body and theheels touching the buttocks
- Keep the knees and feet hip width apart
- Clasp the ankles with your hands
- Inhale, raise the hips, arching the spine
- Keep your feet flat on the floor
- Stay in the position breathing normally
- Exhale and lower the hips down
- Release the ankles and straighten legs to starting position

⚠ **Caution:**

People with ulcers, abdominal hernia, and women in advanced stages of pregnancy should avoid this posture.

✓ **Effects & Benefits:**

This Āsana strengthens the spine, relieves back pain, and helps in correcting rounded shoulders. It expands the chest making the lungs function effectively helping people with breathing difficulties like Asthma, and bronchial problems. It helps to regulate thyroid.

VI-68 Tadāgīmudrā: Pond symbol Posture

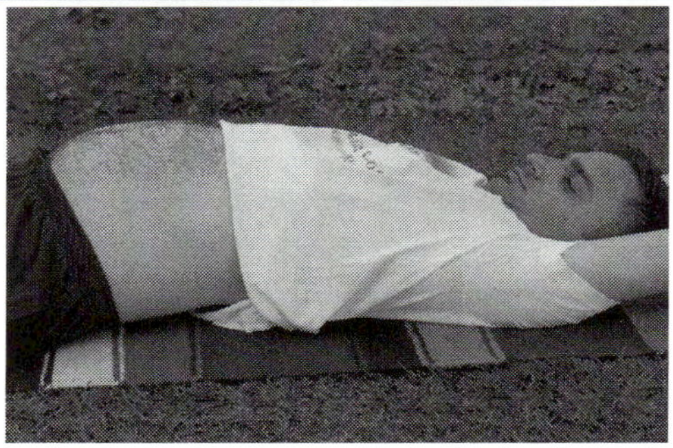

Instructions:

- Lie down on the back, legs together and straight, arms by the sides, palms on the floor and the chin down
- Fold the legs at the knee with the feet on the floor, feet comfortably apart
- Exhale completely and hold the breath with right thumb and index fingers
- Relax the abdomen and then do mock inhalation (act of inhalation with nose closed)
- Feel the cavity formation at abdomen
- Relax the abdomen and release the fingers and slowly
- Inhale, stretch the legs and relax

⚠ **Caution:**

People with abdominal ulcers, hernia, hypertension, heart diseases etc should avoid this posture.

✓ **Effects & Benefits:**

This Āsana improves digestion, removes constipation and tones the respiratory diaphragm.

VI-69 Markatāsana: Monkey Posture

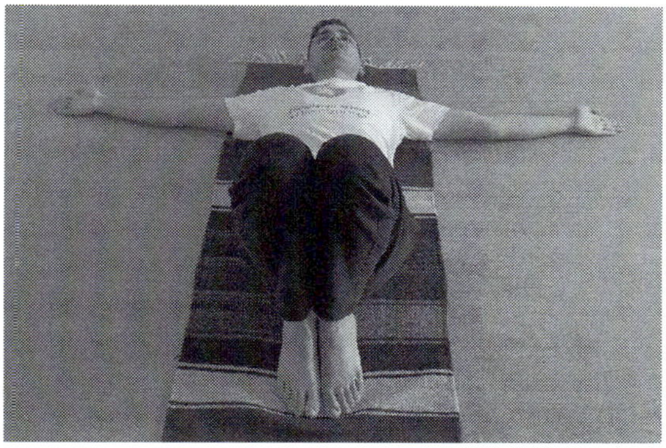

Instructions:

- Lie down on the back, legs together and straight, feet together, arms by the sides, palms on the floor and the chin down
- Bend the legs at the knees and place the feet close to the buttocks
- Inhale, extend the arms to shoulder level, with palms facing up
- Exhale and bring the knees down to the right side, knees touching the floor, simultaneously turning the neck to the left side
- Inhale and bring the knees to the centre
- Exhale and bring the knees to the left side, while turning the neck to the right
- Inhale and bring the knees back to the centre
- Exhale and straighten the legs and bring arms down to the sides
- Practice a few times

⚠ **Caution:**

People with spinal disorders, vertigo and cervical pain may avoid this posture.

✓ **Effects & Benefits:**

This Āsana strengthens the spine and makes it flexible, helps in sciatica, relieves back pain, helps in constipation and aids indigestion.

VI-70 Matsyāsana: Fish Posture

Instructions:

- Lie down on the back, legs together and straight, feet together, arms by the sides, palms on the floor and the chin down
- Inhale and raise your pelvis, with the support of the arms and hands
- Lift the head back to place the top of the head on the floor
- Arch the back and hold the position breathing normally
- Exhale, relax the back and bring the head down to starting position, bringing your arms by the sides

Advanced practitioners:

- Perform the practice with legs in ardha padmāsana position

⚠ **Caution:**

People with cervical pain, back pain, ulcers, hernia and pregnant women should avoid this posture.

✓ **Effects & Benefits:**

This Āsana stimulates the abdominal organs, regulates the thyroid gland and helps to relieve Asthma and bronchial problems.

(Yoga Sutra 2.54)

sva-visayâsamprayoge cittasya svarûpânukâra ivendriyânam pratyâhârah

When our own senses cease to be engaged with the corresponding objects projected by the mind and hence withdraw into the consciousness from which they arose, this is called Pratyāhāra, the fifth step.

Realising that the physical world and the personal world are inextricably connected is important to understand our true self. Our perception of the world is unique and separate from the actual substance the world is made of or how others view it. When we are able to temporarily withdraw from our senses, we will gain a better understanding of this connection which will lead to mastery over the sense organs.

VII Inverted Postures

VII-71 Viparītakarṇī: Inversion Posture

Instructions:

- Lie down on the back, legs together and straight, feet together, arms by the sides, palms on the floor
- Exhale and slowly raise the legs together without bending them and bring them to the horizontal position, taking the legs behind the head
- Lift the buttocks and support the back with palms pointing up and elbows parallel to the floor
- Inhale and lift the legs up vertically keeping the torso about 30 degree inclined
- The weight of the legs should be on the elbows placed on the floor
- Stay in the position breathing normally
- Exhale and bring legs to the horizontal position beyond head
- Inhale and bring arms down to the floor, lowering the hips and legs to the floor

⚠ **Caution:**

People with heart ailments, weak abdominal and back muscles, weak elbow, hypertension, spondylitis and other spinal disorders should avoid this posture.

✓ **Effects & Benefits:**

This Āsana prevents varicose veins disorder, hernia, improves circulation and digestive system.

VII-72 Sarvaṅgāsana: Shoulder stand Posture

Instructions:

- Lie down on the back, legs together and straight, feet together, arms by the sides, palms on the floor
- Exhale and slowly raise both legs together without bending them and come to horizontal position bringing the legs beyond the head
- Lift the buttocks and support the back with palms pointing up and elbows parallel to the floor
- Inhale and straighten the trunk and legs vertically in a straight line with toes facing up
- The weight of the body is supported on the shoulders and chin should be tucked into the chest
- Stay in the position breathing normally
- Exhale and bring the legs to the horizontal position beyond the head
- Inhale and bring the arms down to the floor, lowering the hips and legs to the floor

⚠ Caution:

People with heart ailments, weak abdominal and back muscles, weak elbow, hypertension, spondylitis and other spinal disorders should avoid this posture.

✓ Effects & Benefits:

This Āsana prevents varicose veins, hernia and displacement of organs. It improves circulation and immunity. It stimulates the digestive systems, helps to improve functioning of the brain, works on thyroid and other endocrine glands.

VII-73 Halāsana: Plough Posture

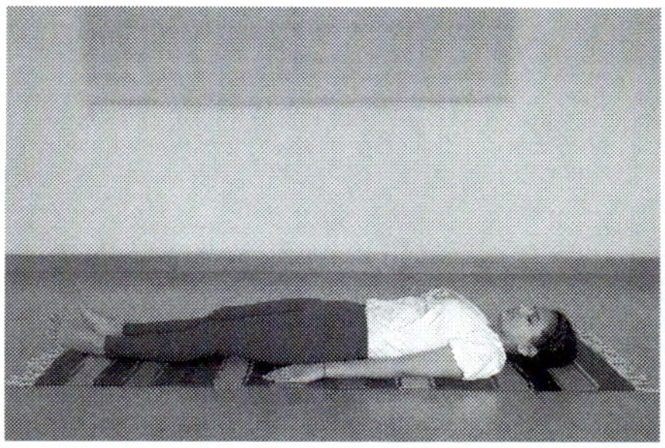
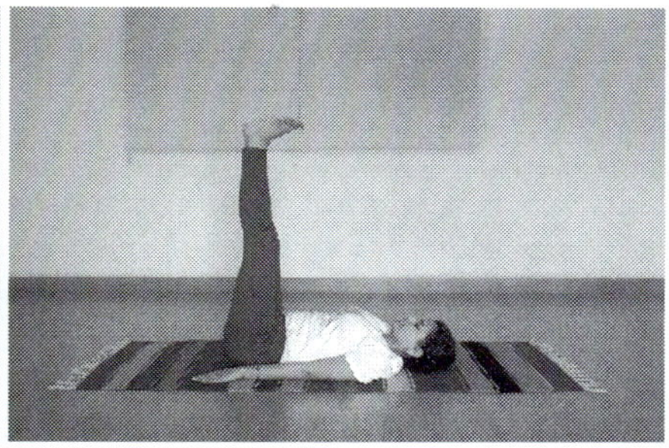

Instructions:

- Lie down on the back, legs together and straight, feet together, arms by the sides, palms on the floor
- Inhale and slowly raise both legs vertically, keeping the trunk in a straight line
- Exhale and lower the legs beyond the head, with the toes touching the floor beyond the head
- Support the back with palms pointing up and elbows parallel to the floor
- Stay in the posture breathing normally
- Inhale and raise both the legs vertically
- Exhale and bring arms down with palms facing floor, gradually lowering hips and legs to the floor

⚠ Caution:

People with heart ailments, weak abdominal and back muscles, weak elbow, hypertension, spondylitis and other spinal disorders should avoid this posture.

✓ Effects & Benefits:

This Āsana Improves circulation and immunity, stimulates the digestive systems, thyroid and other endocrine glands. It helps to improve the functioning of the brain and strengthens the back muscles.

VII-74 Sīrṣāsana/ Bhusīrṣāsana: Head stand Posture

Instructions:

- Sit in Vajrāsana
- Inhale and raise the arms from the front to stand on the knees
- Exhale and bend forward and place forearms on a folded blanket
- Keep fingers interlocked and elbows in front of the knees
- Interlocked palms and elbows should approximately form an equilateral triangle
- Keep the crown of the head near interlocked fingers and wrap hands around the head to fix firmly. This is Bhusirasasan position 1
- Inhale and straighten legs by lifting knees and walk on toes towards the head, bringing the thighs near the chest
- Transfer the body weight towards head and keep lower feet parallel to floor
- This is Bhusirasasan position 2
- Exhale and further lift legs up by the hip joints to bring thighs parallel to the floor
- Slowly move further up with thighs vertical, lower feet folded and back

VII-74 Sīrṣāsana/ Bhusīrṣāsana: Head stand Posture (contd.)

Instructions:

- Adjust the balance to finally straighten the knees to raise lower legs up, legs together
- Adjust position so that body is in a straight line
- Maintain the position breathing normally
- Release the posture in reverse steps and relax in Sashankāsana

⚠ Caution:
People with heart ailments, weak abdominal and back muscles, weak elbow, hypertension, spondylitis and other spinal disorders should avoid this posture.

✓ Effects & Benefits:
This Āsana energises the whole body, helps to improve memory, good for headaches and migraines, stimulates the lymphatic system and relieves stress.

(Yoga Sutra 3.1)

desa-bandhas cittasya dhârañâ

Concentration is the process of holding or fixing the mind's attention onto one object or place, and is the sixth of the eight rungs or limbs. This act is called Dhārana. The mind holds on to an object, either inside or outside the body and keeps itself in that state.

Concentrating on a mantra, intention, or simply clearing and silencing your mind is a way to teach yourself discipline, increase focus, and decrease stress.

VIII Prone Postures

VIII-75 Advāsana: Prone Posture/Reverse corpse Posture

Instructions:

- This posture is the reverse of Savāāsana and is called the reverse corpse posture
- Lie prone on the stomach, with legs straight and apart, feet apart and arms by the side of the body
- Raise your arms above the head to place them on the floor, palms close together and facing down
- The whole body should be straight and aligned
- The forehead should touch the ground
- Relax the whole body and take deep breaths, focussing on each part of the body
- Stay in this position, breathing deeply to relax completely

✓ Effects & Benefits:

The posture is very good for people having back problems, it removes stress, removes stiffness from the body by giving a good stretch for the whole body, it nourishes the abdominal organs and is found to be helpful in depression

VIII-76 Makarāsana: Crocodile Posture

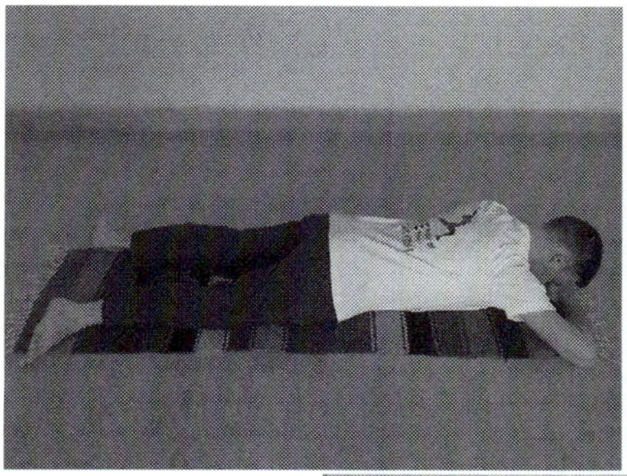

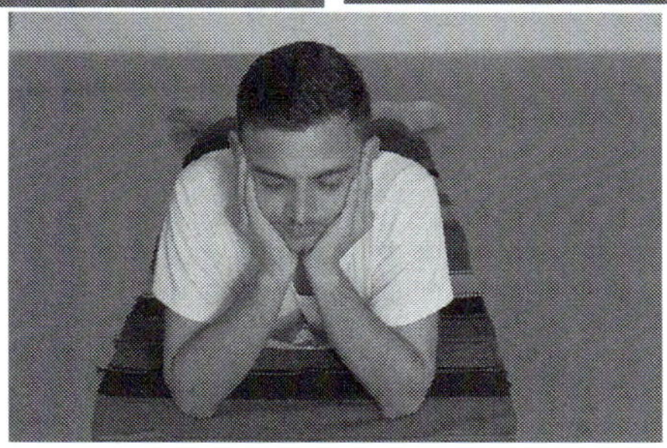

Instructions:

- Lie prone on the stomach, with legs straight and apart, feet apart and arms by the side of the body
- Raise your arms above the head to place them on the floor, palms facing down
- Inhale, raise the head and shoulders bringing your arms up to hold the chin in the palms of the hands
- Elbows should be on the ground
- Stay in this position breathing normally
- Exhale and bring the head and shoulders down, keeping the forehead on the floor and arms by the sides

⚠ Caution:

People having pronounced lumbar curve should avoid this posture.

✓ Effects & Benefits:

This Āsana is very good for people having sciatica, slipped disc, hypertension, stress and anxiety. It stimulates the abdominal organs and helps to function effectively.

VIII-77 Bhujaṅgāsana: Cobra Posture

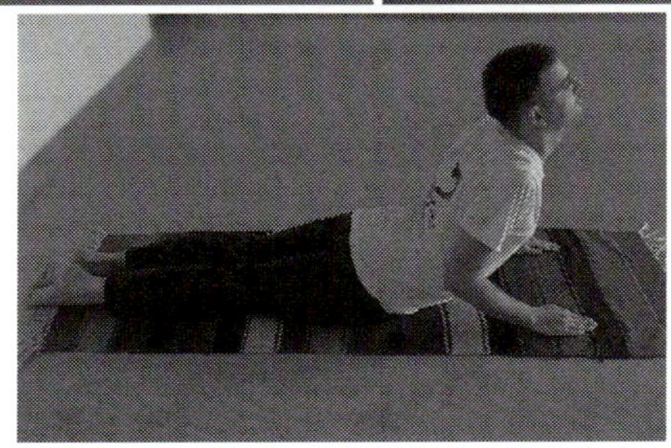

Instructions:

- Lie prone on the stomach, forehead on the floor, with legs straight and together, feet turned out, arms by the side of the body
- The body should be aligned in a straight line
- Bend elbows to place the palms near the chest, elbows pointing back and fingers pointing in the front
- Inhale and raise your chest, shoulders and head
- Stay in this position breathing normally
- Exhale and lower head, shoulders, chest and forehead to the floor

⚠ **Caution:**

People having hernia, ulcers and pregnant women should avoid this posture.

✓ **Effects & Benefits:**

This Āsana strengthens the spine, stimulates all organs in the abdominal region to function effectively. It alleviates back pain, neck pain, helps in cervical spondylitis, helps in digestive problems, and removes constipation.

VIII-78 Tiryaka Bhujangāsana: Twisting cobra Posture

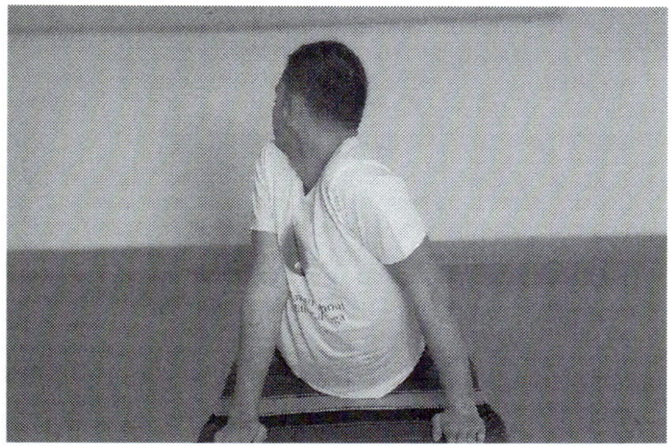

Instructions:

- Lie down on the stomach, forehead on the floor, your legs and feet slightly apart, feet turned out, arms by the sides of the body and toes tucked in
- Bend elbows to place palms on the floor near the chest, close to the body
- Inhale, press the palms and raise your chest, shoulders and head
- Straighten the elbows raising the upper torso
- Exhale and twist the head and upper torso to the right to look at the left heel
- The arms should be straight or bent very slightly
- Stay in this position breathing normally
- Inhale and slowly bring the head to the centre
- Exhale and twist the head and upper torso to the left to look at the right heel
- Stay in the position breathing normally
- Inhale and slowly bring the head back to the centre
- Exhale, lower head, shoulder, chest, and forehead to the floor

⚠ **Caution:**

People with wrist, arms, shoulder injury, hernia, ulcers and pregnant women should avoid this posture.

✓ **Effects & Benefits:**

This Āsana strengthens the spine and makes it flexible. It stimulates and tones the abdomen and abdominal organs, improves digestion and strengthens arms and shoulders.

VIII-79 Ardha Śalabhāsana: Half Locust Posture - Variation 1

Instructions:

- Lie down on the stomach, forehead on the floor, your legs straight and together, feet turned out and arms by the sides of the body
- Raise your arms above the head to place them on the floor, with palms turned down and chin on the floor
- Inhale, raise the right leg, simultaneously raising the head, chest and left arm
- Keep the legs and arms straight
- Stay in the position breathing normally
- Exhale and lower the right leg, head, chest and left arm to the floor
- Repeat the same with left leg and right arm

⚠ **Caution:**

People with severe back pain, sciatica, and disc prolapse should avoid this posture.

✓ **Effects & Benefits:**

This Āsana strengthens the entire spine, tones the back muscles, and strengthens the upper and lower back.

VIII-79a Ardha Śalabhāsana - Variation 2

Instructions:

- Lie down on the stomach, forehead on the floor, your legs straight and together, feet turned out and arms by the sides of the body
- Make fists of the hands and place them under the thighs with chin on the floor
- Inhale and raise your right leg, ensuring the left leg is straight and firmly on the floor
- Stay in the position breathing normally
- Exhale and bring the right leg down
- Repeat the same with the left leg

⚠ **Caution:**

People with severe back pain, sciatica, and disc prolapse should avoid this posture.

✓ **Effects & Benefits:**

This Āsana strengthens the entire spine, tones the back muscles, and strengthens upper and lower back.

VIII-80 Śalabhāsana: Locust Posture

Instructions:

- Lie down on the stomach, forehead on the floor, your legs straight and together, feet turned out and arms by the sides of the body
- Make fists of the hands and place them under the thighs, with chin on the floor
- Inhale and raise both legs up keeping them straight and together
- Stay in this position breathing normally
- Exhale and bring both legs down to the floor

Variation:

- Lie down on the stomach, forehead on the floor, your legs straight and together, feet turned out and arms by the sides of the body
- Inhale and sweep arms above the head, simultaneously raising legs, chest and head
- The legs should be straight and knees off the floor
- Stay in the position breathing normally
- Exhale and lower your head, chest and legs to the floor, bringing the arms to the sides of the body

VIII-80 Śalabhāsana: Locust Posture (contd.)

⚠ Caution:
People having heart problem, high blood pressure, ulcers, severe back pain, and sciatica should avoid this posture.

✓ Effects & Benefits:
This Āsana helps in alleviating back pain, stimulates and tones the abdominal organs, helps in digestion, relieves bloating, strengthens the spine and makes it flexible.

VIII-81 Dhanurāsana: Bow Posture

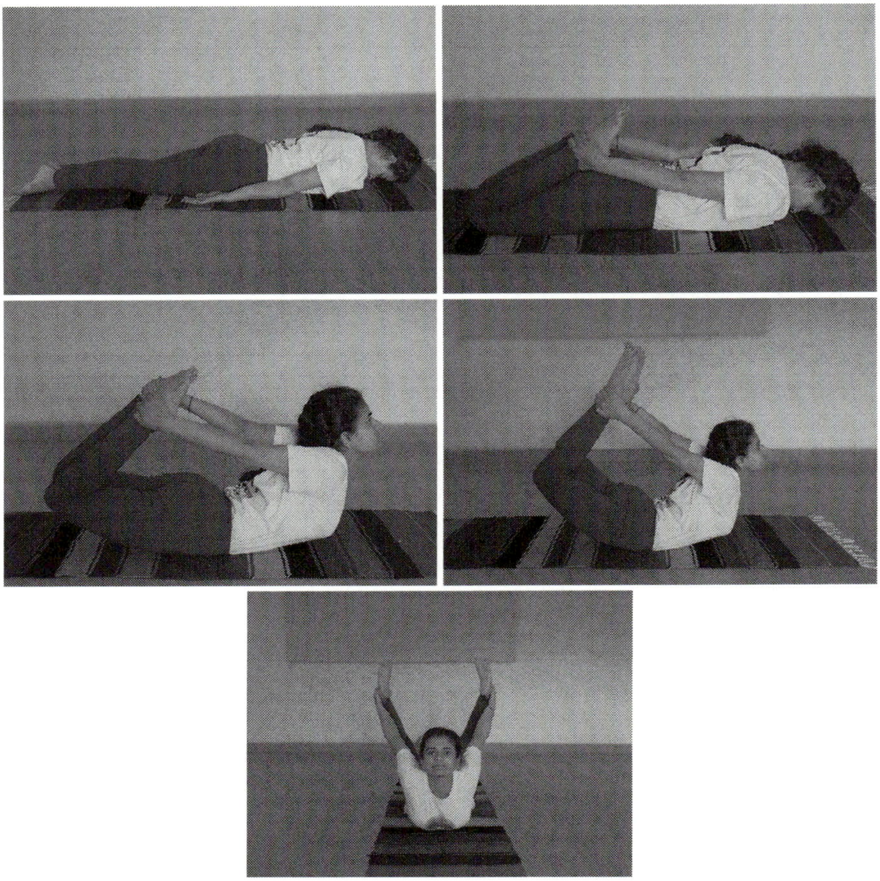

Instructions:

- Lie down on the stomach, forehead on the floor, your legs straight and together, feet turned out, arms by the sides of the body and palms facing up
- Inhale, bend the knees and hold your ankles, keeping the forehead on the floor andfeet and knees together
- Exhale in this position
- Inhale and pull the feet back simultaneously raising the thighs, chest and head
- Knees should be off the floor, head arched back and the whole body supported by the abdomen
- Stay in the position breathing normally
- Exhale and lower head, chest and knees to the floor
- Inhale in this position
- Exhale and then release ankles, straighten legs and bring arms to the sides of the body

VIII-81 Dhanurāsana: Bow Posture (contd.)

⚠ Caution:

People having heart ailments, blood pressure, ulcers and hernia should avoid this posture.

✓ Effects & Benefits:

This Āsana stimulates and tones the abdominal organs to function effectively. It strengthens the back, helps in lung related problems, aids digestion, corrects posture and reduces abdominal fat.

VIII-82 Aśtānga Namaskārāsana: Eight-pointed Prayer Posture

Instructions:

- From Parvatāsana, hold your breath to lower the knees, chest, chin and feet to the floor
- Eight parts of the body are now touching the floor, i.e. toes, knees, hands, chest and chin
- The hips, abdomen and buttocks are raised
- Hold your breath for a few seconds

⚠ **Caution:**

People with back problems, heart problems, weak wrists, hypertension, as well as pregnant women should avoid this posture.

✓ **Effects & Benefits:**

This Āsana strengthens the legs and arms, and improves spine flexibility.

(Yoga Sutra 3.2)

tatra pratyayaika-tânatâ dhyânam

The uninterrupted stream of one point of focus is called absorption in meditation or Dhyāna and is the seventh of the eight limbs. Dhyāna is an important aspect of yoga that is often thought of as separate or optional. However, it is a valuable tool and a way to grow your understanding and practice of yoga.

IX Sūrya Namaskār

Sūrya Namaskār consists of a series of twelve postures as below.

1. Pranāmāsana

2. Hasta Uthānāsana

3. Pādahastāsana

4. Aśva sañchalanāsana

5. Parvatāsana

6. Aśtānga Namaskārāsana

7. Bhujaṅgāsana

8. Parvatāsana

9. Aśva sañchalanāsana

10. Pādahastāsana

11. Hasta Uthānāsana

12. Pranāmāsana

Note: Start the practice with the right side and complete the above sequence to finish half round. This is then followed by repeating the practice on the left side (i.e. take the left leg back for Aśva sañchalanāsana and continue further), so as to complete one round.

After completion of each half round, if required, you can lower the arms to the sides and concentrate on the breathing till it becomes normal. You can continue the practice after that.

You may repeat the practice for three to six rounds as per your capacity. However, avoid strain at all times and look at increasing the repetitions gradually.

Mantras related to the Sun Salutations

1. **Om Mitrāya Namaha**, Salutations to the friend of all.
2. **Om Rayave Namaha**, Salutations to the shining one.
3. **Om Suryāya Namaha**, Salutations to he who induces activity.
4. **Om Bhānave Namaha**, Salutations to he who illumines.
5. **Om Khagāya Namaha**, Salutations to he who moves quickly in the Sky.
6. **Om Pushne Namaha**, Salutations to the giver of strength.
7. **Om Hiranya Garbhāya Namaha**, Salutations to the golden, cosmic self.
8. **Om Marīchaye Namaha**, Salutations to the Lord of the Dawn.
9. **Om Adityāya Namaha**, Salutations to the son of Aditi, the cosmic mother.
10. **Om Sāvitre Namaha**, Salutations to the lord of creation.
11. **Om Arkāya Namaha**, Salutations to he who is fit to be praised.
12. **Om Bhāskarāya Namaha**, Salutations to he who leads to enlightenment.

(Yoga Sutra 3.3)

tad evârtha-mâtra-nirbhâsam svarûpa-sûnyam iva samâdhih

When only the essence of that object, place, or point of focus shines forth in the mind, that deep concentration is called Samādhi, which is the eighth limb or rung.

Achieving a state of deep concentration leading to samādhi may take practice and focus, but it will lead you to new ways of thinking and to revelations about yourself and your perspective on the world.

X Prānāyāma

X-1 Yogic breathing

Instructions:

Abdominal breathing:

- Sit in a comfortable cross-legged position
- Keep the back and spine erect, placing the palms on the thighs comfortably
- Close the eyes and relax the body
- Adopt cin mudrā by making contact at tips of respective index fingers and thumbs
- Feel the breathing mainly at the lower part of lungs with abdominal breathing
- Feel the abdomen moving a little forward and sinking back each time
- Continue for 7 to 10 rounds

Thoracic breathing:

- Adopt Cinmaya mudrā by closing little, ring and middle fingers and feel the breathing. Keep the tips of index and thumb fingers in contact.
- By movements of costal inter costal muscles at thoracic region, feel the diametrical expansion and contraction at thoracic region during inhalation and exhalation
- Feel breathing mainly at the middle one third portion of lungs
- Continue for 7 to 10 rounds of breathing

Clavicle breathing:

- Place thumb on palm and close with the other four fingers
- Feel the breathing mainly at the top one third part of lungs
- Inhale and move the shoulders a little up and backward
- Exhale and move the shoulders a little down and forward
- Continue for 7 to 10 rounds of breathing

Complete yogic breathing:

- Combine all the 3 sectional breathings
- Keep palms at navel region making a fist with thumb inside
- Inhale with abdominal, thoracic, and abdominal muscles and exhale in the same order.
- Continue for 7 to 10 rounds of breathing.

Effects & Benefits:

This Prāṇāyāma helps to relieve anxiety, tension, calms the mind and helps to reduce psychosomatic disorders.

X-2 Kapālabhāti Kriyā (Kriya / Purification)

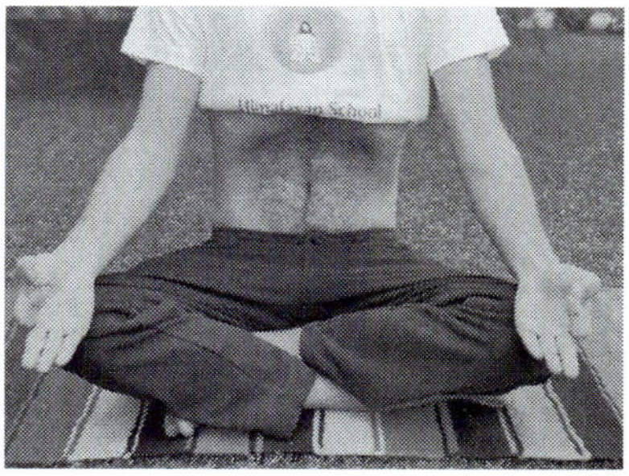

Instructions:

- Sit in any comfortable posture of choice (Ardhapadmāāsana/Padmāāsana) or Sukhāāsana
- Keep the back, neck and head erect
- Place hands in cin or Jñana mudrā
- Keep your eyes closed
- Kapālbhāti is a respiratory kriya practice with exhalation active and inhalation passive and automatic
- Exhale forcibly with a sound using abdominal muscles
- While inhaling silently, the abdomen should return to its original position
- One inhale/exhale is one round
- Repeat at least 15 to 30 rounds.
- Relax for a while and start the next cycle
- Try to practice 5 to 10 cycles, but it is important to pause between two cycles and feel the stillness of mind

⚠ **Caution:**

If pain or dizziness is experienced, stop the practice and relax for some time. Resume the practice with more awareness and less force.

Those suffering from heart disease, high blood pressure, gastritis, vertigo or hernia should not practice Kapālbhāti. This kriya should be practised with attention in a rhythmic slow speed.

Important: Every round should begin with an exhalation and should end with an inhalation.

✓ **Effects & Benefits:**

This technique enables in eliminating large amounts of toxins contained in the body. This kriya clears the nasal cavities and lungs, stimulates the abdominal organs and activates brain cells.

It brings relief from asthma and tones the abdominal muscles and helps to develop concentration. It purifies the Idā and Pingala nādis and removes sensory distractions from the mind. It energizes the body, stimulates the mind, removes lethargy and prepares mind for meditation.

X-3 Bhastrika Prānāyāma

Instructions:

- Sit in a comfortable position, keeping the spine erect, hands on the knees in cin or jňana mudrā
- Inhale deeply and forcefully
- Exhale forcefully through the nose
- Repeat the forceful inhalation and exhalation
- Keep up the rapid breathing for 10 to 15 breaths
- Take a deep breath and rest
- Repeat the cycle 5 times
- The breathing should be rhythmic, and the proportion of inhalation and exhalation should be equal

⚠ **Caution:**

People with heart problems, blood pressure, hernia, epilepsy, retinal issues and vertigo should not practise Bhastrika.

✓ **Effects & Benefits:**

This Prānāyāma flushes out carbon dioxide and toxins from the body. It removes phlegm, tones the digestive system and balances the three doṣās - vāta (wind), pitta (bile) and kapha (phlegm).

X-4 Ujjai Prānāyāma

Instructions:

- Sit in a comfortable position, keeping the spine erect and body relaxed
- Bring your focus on the throat
- Slightly constrict the throat (the glottis) and inhale and exhale
- There will be a slight hissing sound produced through the throat as one inhales and exhales
- The sound should be very subtle
- The inhale and exhale should be smooth without disruption
- Practice for 10 to 12 breaths

⚠ **Caution:**

People having throat infections may avoid this prānāyāma.

✓ **Effects & Benefits:**

This Prānāyāma soothes the nervous system, calms the mind and helps to prevent thyroid disorders.

X-5 Candra Bhedana:

Instructions:

- Sit in a comfortable position (Ardhapadmāsana/ Padmāsana) or Sukhāsana with spine erect
- Place hands on knees in cin or Jňana mudrā
- Bend the forefinger and middle finger of the right hand in Nāsāgra mudrā
- Inhale through the left nostril closing the right nostril with the right thumb
- Exhale through the right nostril closing the left nostril with the ring and little finger
- The inhale and exhale should be slow, steady and deep
- Repeat for 10 breaths

⚠ **Caution:**

People with blocked nostrils,cough and cold should avoid this practice.

✓ **Effects & Benefits:**

The Prāṇāyāma helps to reduce sinusitis, tension headaches, and colds. It helps in calming the mind and helps people suffering from insomnia.

X-6 Sūrya Bhedana:

Instructions:

- Sit in a comfortable position (Ardhapadmāsana/Padmāsana or Sukhāāsana) with spine erect
- Place hands on knees in chin or Jňana mudrā
- Bend the forefinger and middle finger of the right hand in Nāsāgra mudrā
- Inhale through right nostril closing the left nostril with ring and little finger
- Exhale through left nostril closing the right nostril with thumb
- Inhale and exhale should be slow, steady and deep
- Repeat for 10 breaths

⚠ **Caution:**

People with heart disease and high blood pressure should avoid this Prānāyāma.

✓ **Effects & Benefits:**

This Prānāyāma activates the pingala nādi and helps to energise the body. It makes the mind more alert, gets rid of dullness and lethargy and helps to reduce depression.

X-7 Nādī Śodana(Nādi Shuddhi / Anuloma Viloma- Alternate nostril breathing)

Instructions:

- Sit in any comfortable posture of choice (Ardhapadmāāsana/Padmāāsana) or Sukhāāsana)
- Fold the forefinger and middle finger of the right hand
- Place the thumb above the right nostril and the ring and little finger above the left
- These 2 fingers control the flow of breath in the nostril by alternately pressing on one nostril, blocking the flow of breath with the other finger
- Same technique is repeated with the other nostril
- Inhale through left nostril closing the right nostril with thumb
- Exhale through right nostril by removing the thumb and closing the left nostril with the ring finger
- Inhale through right nostril closing left nostril with ring finger
- Exhale through left nostril closing the right nostril with thumb
- This is one round of Nādī Śodana
- Continue to do 10 rounds

X-7 Nādī Śodana(Nādi Shuddhi / Anuloma Viloma- Alternate nostril breathing) (contd.)

⚠ Caution:
One should not practice while having cold, cough or fever.

✓ Effects & Benefits:
This practice purifies the Nādīs and Cakrās. Asthma and nasal allergies can be contained by doing this practice. It reduces anxiety and stress, helps in developing concentration and enables mind to focus. Long standing practice of Nādī Śodana helps to bring balance and equanimity in life.

X-8 Śītali Prānāyāma

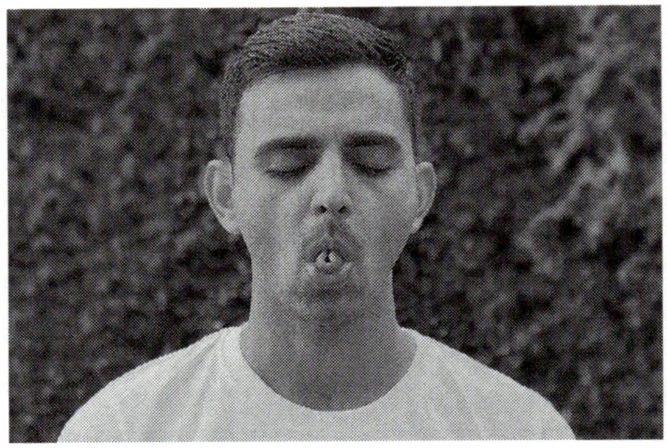

Instructions:

- Sit in a comfortable position
- Keep the back and spine erect
- Roll the sides of the tongue to form a tube
- Protrude the curled tongue from the lips
- Inhale through the rolled tongue with a sound similar to drinking through a straw
- Take the tongue in, close the lips and breathe out through both nostrils
- Repeat for 10 breaths

⚠ **Caution:**

People with low blood pressure or having respiratory problems should avoid this Prānāyāma.

✓ **Effects & Benefits:**

This Prānāyāma cools the body, activates the liver, makes the mind calm and peaceful and improves digestion.

X-9 Sītkari Prāṇāyāma

Instructions:

- Sit in a comfortable position
- Keep the back and spine erect
- Slightly part the lips and bring both upper and lower teeth together
- Fold the tongue and keep it between the jaws
- Inhale slowly through the mouth
- Close the lips relax the tongue and exhale through both nostrils
- Repeat the same process for 10 breaths

⚠ **Caution:**

People with low blood pressure or having respiratory problems should avoid this Prāṇāyāma.

✓ **Effects & Benefits:**

This Prāṇāyāma cools the body, activates the liver, makes the mind calm and peaceful and improves digestion.

X-10 Bhrāmari Prānāyāma

 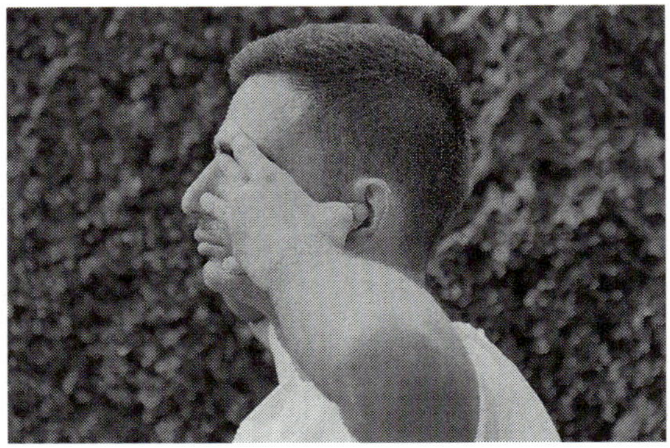

Instructions:

- Sit in a comfortable position
- Keep the back and spine erect
- Close the eyes and relax the body
- Raise your arms from the sides with elbows pointing sideways
- Place the thumbs at the openings of the ears, index fingers on the eyes, middle fingers at the nostrils, ring fingers above lips and little fingers below the mouth. This is also known as ṣanmukhi mudrā
- Inhale slowly and deeply through the nose
- Exhale slowly with the humming sound of a bee
- Repeat for 10 breaths

✓ **Effects & Benefits:**

This Prānāyāma helps to relieve anxiety and tension. It calms the mind, helps people suffering from blood pressure, migraines and helps to build concentration.

XI Bandhas

XI - Tri bandha- Mūlabandha, Jalandharbandha & Udyanābandha

Instructions:

Mūlabandha:

- Sit in a comfortable cross-legged meditative posture
- Keep your eyes closed
- Gently contract and pull up the pelvic floor at perineum
- Maintain for 10 breaths and release pelvic floor

Jalandharabandha:

- Sit in a comfortable cross-legged meditative posture
- Keep your eyes closed
- Exhale completely and without inhaling air, take the chin to chest between collar bones and windpipe is closed
- Maintain as per capacity to hold air outside
- Slowly remove the bandha and inhale

XI - Tri bandha- Mūlabandha, Jalandharbandha & Udyanābandha (contd.)

Instructions:

Udyānabandha and Tri bandha:

- Sit in a comfortable cross-legged meditative posture
- Keep your eyes closed
- Apply Mūlabandha
- Apply Jalandharabandha
- After applying Jalandharbandha relax the abdominal muscles and expand the chest
- Do mock inhalation without any air going inside by raising the respiratory diaphragm up
- Maintain as per capacity for a few seconds
- Inhale and release the abdominal muscles and chin slowly

Note: Bandhas are neuro muscular locks applied in the body to channelize the Prana Shakti. In general Bandhas and Mudrās are applied as part of prānāyāma.

⚠ **Caution:**
People with hypertension, heart ailments or any abdominal thoracic disorders should avoid the Tri bandha.

✓ **Effects & Benefits:**
Bandhas channelize the prāna and awaken the energy centres. It helps to improve functions of various body systems such as endocrine systems, digestive systems and excretory systems.

XII Mudrās

The word Mudrā means symbol or gesture. Mudrās are blissful neuro-muscular contacts of body parts for channelizing the prana shakti. Initially mudrās are used to bring awareness of the flow of Prana in the body. Mudrās can be used to control the dissipation of Prana from the body and to contain it within.

Mudrās can be introduced during Āsana and Prāṇāyāma practice or after Āsana and Prāṇāyāma. Following are some of the main mudrās (gestures) used in prāṇāyāma and meditation.

Cin Mudrā

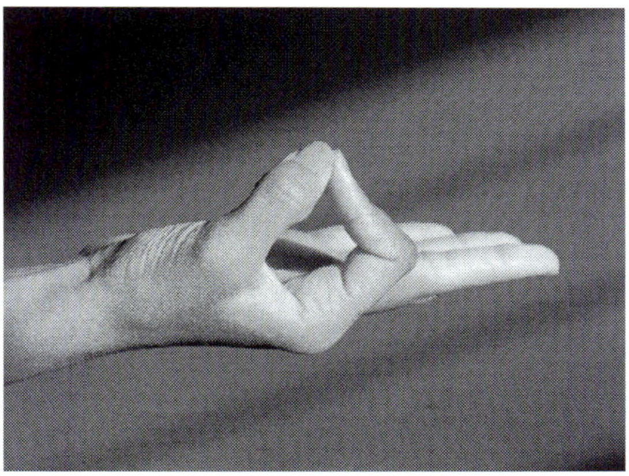

- Sit comfortably in any cross-legged position with back straight
- Keep your palms on your thighs near the knees with palms facing upwards
- Make contact of the tip of your index finger and thumb on each hand
- Keep other 3 fingers straight

✓ Effects:

Cin mudrā helps to improve concentration and is a gesture of knowledge. It helps in relaxation and abdominal breathing.

Jnāna Mudrā

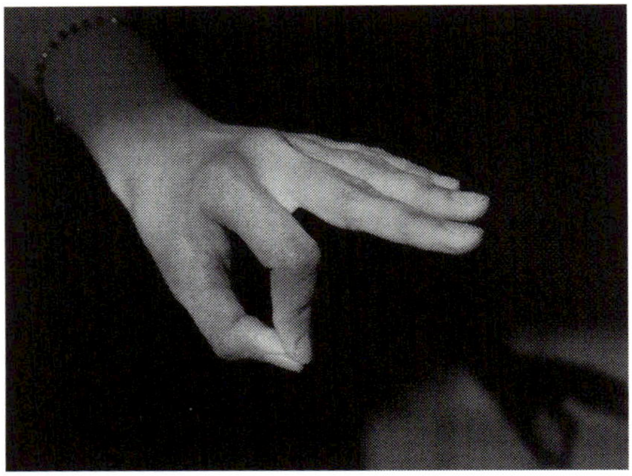

- Sit comfortably in any cross-legged position with the back straight
- Keep your palms on your thighs near the knees with the palms facing downwards
- Make contact of the tip of your index finger and thumb on each hand
- Keep the other 3 fingers straight

✓ **Effects:**
This mudrā symbolizes knowledge. It unites elements of fire and air representing joining of Self and universal consciousness.

Prānamudrā

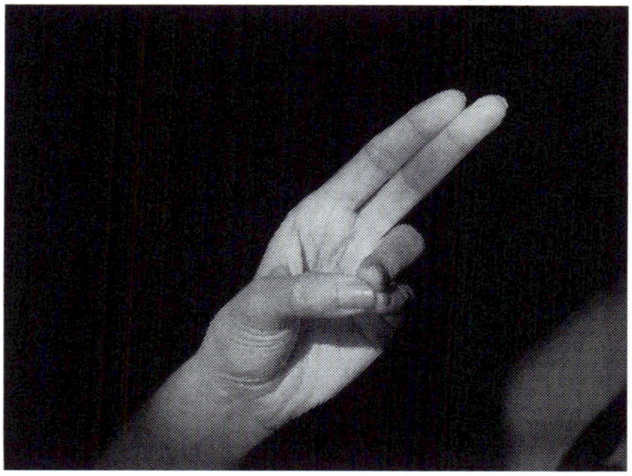 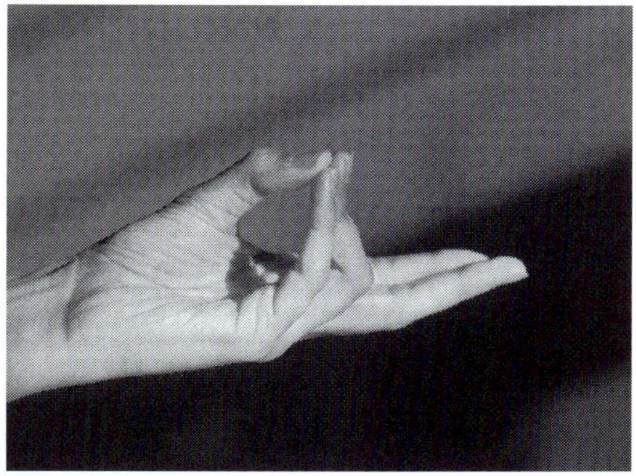

- Sit comfortably in any cross-legged position with the back straight
- Keep your palms on your thighs near the knees with palms facing upwards
- Make contact of the tips of your thumbs with the tips of your ring finger and little finger on each hand
- Keep the other 2 fingers straight
- This symbolizes balancing of water and earth elements of the body

Effects:
It is supposed to reduce tiredness and rejuvenate the whole system.

Khecarimudrā

- Sit comfortably in any cross-legged position with the back straight
- Keep your palms on your thighs near the knees with palms cupping the knees or in Chin mudrā or Jnana mudrā
- Keep the eyes closed
- Stretch the tip of the tongue to back side of the soft palate and roll back further to the extent possible
- Maintain for 10 breaths
- Release the tongue and relax
- Feel the silence of mind
- Open your eyes

Note: Any mouth ailments are contra indicated

✓ **Effects:**

This mudrā stimulates many nerve centers and stimulates secretion of hormones. It helps in mental calmness and prevention of psychosomatic disorders.

Kākimudrā

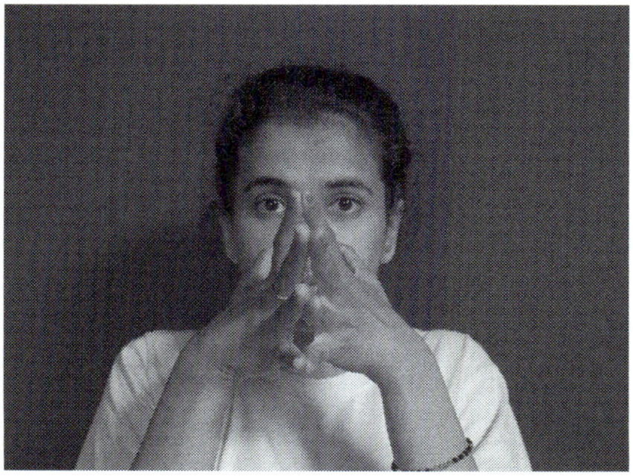

- Sit comfortably in cross-legged posture with the spine erect
- Close your eyes and relax the body
- Open your eyes and keep the focus of your eyes on the tip of nose without blinking
- Form abeak shape with the lips and inhale through the beak
- Close the mouth
- Exhale through the nose
- Continue for 7 to 10 rounds

Benefits:
Kāki mudrā is a relaxing practice and helps to remove fatigue and stress. This also helps to prevent psychosomatic disorders

Ṣanmukhīmudrā

- Sit comfortably in a cross-legged posture with the spine erect
- Close your eyes and relax the body
- Place your thumbs on your ears, index fingers over your eyes, middle fingers over the nose, your ring fingers over the upper lip and your little fingers over the lower lips symbolically closing all sense organs.
- Do normal breathing through the nose for 10 rounds

✓ **Benefits:**
This is a relaxing practice and helps in prevention of psychosomatic disorders.

XIII ILLUSTRATIVE YOGA SCHEDULES

In this chapter, we present a few yoga schedules that can be practised at home. Before you commence practice, please refer to the general guidelines for āsana and prāṇāyāma mentioned at the start of the book. Further, if you have any ailments, please consult a physician and obtain advice before practising the schedules below.

Yoga Schedule for Beginners

The below mentioned schedule can be followed by beginners, i.e. those with limited or no prior experience in yoga.

Week 1

Light Yogic Exercises

Asanas

1. Setubandhāsana
2. Pavanamuktāsana
3. Bhujaṅgāsana
4. Ardha Śalabhāsana

Rest

5. Tādāsana
6. Tiryak Tādāsana
7. Kati Cakrāsana
8. Vīrabhadrāsana
9. Śaśāṅkāsana
10. Tadasana
11. Triyak Tadasana
12. Mārjārāsana
13. Yogāsana

Rest

Prāṇāyāma

1. Yogic breathing - 10 Breaths

Note:

- Beginners can start with two to three repetitions of each asana and progressively build it up with regular practice.
- It is a good practice to end the yoga session with Shavasana and a short meditation. This is, of course, dependent on time availability of the individual

Week 2

Light Yogic Exercises

Kriya

1. Kapālabhāti - 15/15/15 times with breaks in between each round

Asanas

1. Bhujaṅgāsana
2. Tiryak Bhujaṅgāsana
3. Ardha Śalabhāsana - variation
4. Markatāsana
5. Ardha Pavanamuktāsana

Rest

6. Tādāsana
7. Tiryak Tādāsana
8. Kati Cakrāsana
9. Pādahastāsana
10. Trikoṇāsana
11. Uthana Maṇdukāsana
12. Baddhakōnāsana

Rest

Pranayama

Ujjai Breathing - 10 Breaths

Week 3

Light Yogic Exercises

Kriya

1. Kapālabhāti - 20/20/20 Times with breaks in between each round

Asanas

1. Tādāsana
2. Vīrabhadrāsana 2
3. Pādahastāsana
4. Vṛkṣāsana
5. Pādahastāsana
6. Aśvasañcalanāsana
7. Parvatāsana <perform 5, 6, and 7 together>
8. Trikoṇāsana Parivrtti -Twist

Rest

9. Mārjārāsana
10. Bhūnamanāsana
11. Jānu Śīrṣāsana
12. Maṇḍūkāsana

Rest

13. Śalabhāsana
14. Markatāsana
15. Naukāsana

Rest

Pranayama

16. Bastrika - 10 Breaths

Week 4

Light Yogic Exercises

Kriya

1. Kapālabhāti - 30/30/30 Times with breaks in between each round

Asanas

1. Tādāsana
2. Tiryak Tādāsana variation
3. Sūryanamaskār 2-3 rounds to begin with
4. Ardha Utkatāsana
5. Prasārita Pāda Utthānāsana

Rest

6. Śalabhāsana variation
7. Makarāsana
8. Advāsana
9. Supta Baddha Kōnāsana
10. Setubandhāsana
11. Urdhva Prasarita Pādāsana

Rest

12. Vakrāsana
13. Paścimottāsana

Rest

Prānāyāma

14. Śītali/Śītkari 10 breaths

Yoga Schedule for Intermediate to Advanced Practice

The sequences below are slightly more challenging and should be attempted by those with sufficient prior practice in yoga. At the very minimum, they should have completed the previous schedules for beginners and should have attained a level of comfort with those practices.
As mentioned in the Guidelines at the start of the book, there should be no pain in any part of the body during the practice. Please stop the practice if discomfort persists, and attempt it later after more practice. In case of continuing discomfort, do consult a physician or a senior yoga teacher to assist you.

Practitioner should begin with light yogic exercises and Kapālabhāti kriya as before, in order to prepare the body for the strenuous practices in these schedules.

—— ◆ ——

Week 1

Asanas

---

1. Tādāsana
2. Utthānāsana
3. Natarājāsana
4. Pārśvakoṇāsana - Lateral
5. Sūryanamaskāram (4-6 rounds)

Rest

---

6. Vyāghrasāna
7. Navāsana
8. Ardha Uṣtrāsana
9. Gomukhāsana
10. Upaviṣtakōṇāsana

Rest

---

11. Tiryak Bhujaṅgāsana
12. Ardha Śalabhāsana
13. Skandharāsana
14. Supta Pādāṅguṣtāsana

Rest

Prāṇāyāma

15. Śītali/Śītkari 10 breaths.

—— ◆ ——

Week 2

Asanas

---

1. Tādāsana
2. Vīrabhadrāsana III
3. Pārśva Uttanāsana
4. Utkatāsana
5. Uttāna Pṛṣtāsana

Rest

---

6. Ardha Śalabhāsana – Variation
7. Dhanurāsana
8. Supta Prasārita Pādāṅguṣṭāsana
9. Viparītakarṇi
10. Pavanamuktāsana without neck movement

Rest

---

11. Uṣtrāsana
12. Simhāsana
13. Ardhamatsyendrāsana
14. Pascimōttānāsana

Rest

Prāṇāyāma

15. Chandra Bhedana - 10 breaths.

Week 3

Asanas

1. Tādāsana
2. Vīrabhadrāsana III
3. Udhita Hasta Pādāṅguṣṭāsana
4. Ardhacandrāsana
5. Pārśvakoṇāsana - Parivrtti (Twist)

Rest

6. Maṇḍūkāsana
7. Catuṣpāda pītham
8. Mārjārāsana
9. Supta Vajrāsana

Rest

10. Supta Pādāngustāsana
11. Sarvāṅgāsana
12. Matsyāsana
13. Markatāsana
14. Pavanamuktāsana (without lifting head)

Rest

Prāṇāyāma

15. Sūrya Bhedana – 10 Breaths.

Week 4

Asanas

1. Tādāsana
2. Pārśva Uttānāsana
3. Garudāsana
4. Vīrabhadrāsana-1
5. Uttānāsana
6. Trikoṇāsana – Lateral
7. Sūryanamaskāram

Rest

8. Pūrvatanāsana
9. Paścimōttānāsana
10. Ūrdhva Prasṛta Pādāsana
11. Sarvāṅgāsana
12. Halāsana
13. Markatāsana
14. Pavanamuktāsana

Rest

Prānāyāma

15. Nādī Śodhana - 10 Breaths.
16. Bhrāmari - 10 Breaths.

TRANSLITERATION SCHEME FOR READING SANSKRIT WORDS IN ENGLISH

Vowels

Letter with diacritic	Pronounciation as per Devanagari script	Words to be pronounced
a	**a**	amba, ambika, akaraha
ā	**aa**	aakasaha, aagraha, aanandaha, aadityaha
i	**e**	enduhu, endira, estaha, eehitaha, eelitaha
ī	**ee**	eeshaha, eeha, eehitaha, eelitaha
u	**u**	uttara, udaram, udattaha, udi
ū	**uu**	uusha, uuha, uuruhu
ṛ	**ru**	rutu, rutam, runam, russihi
ḷ	**Lu**	Kluptam
e	**ë**	ëkaha, ëkantaha, ëkadashi, ëshaha
ai	**ai**	aikyam, aichath, airavatam, ailaha
o	**o**	omkaraha, ojaha, ojaswi
au	**au**	audaryam, audumbaram, aushmyam
ṃ	**am**	mukham, vadanam, shareeram
aḥ	**Ha**	vrukshaha, parvataha, manushyaha

Consonants

ka	kha	ga	gha	ṅga
ca	cha	ja	jha	ñja
ṭa	ṭha	ḍa	ḍha	ṇa
ta	tha	da	dha	na
pa	pha	ba	bha	ma
ya	ra	la	va	

ś(s)	ṣ (sh)	sa ha
kṣa	tra	jña

ka-	katha, katham, kadā, kadanam, kanakam
kha-	khataḥ, khaṭana, khagaḥ, nakham
ga-	gaganam, gaṅgā, gajaḥ, gaṇitam
gha-	ghaṭaḥ, ghōṭakaḥ, ghōraḥ, ghōtí
ṅga-	pataṅgaḥ

ca-	candanam, candraḥ, caritaḥ, calanam
cha-	chādanam, chādaḥ chātraḥ, chatram
ja-	jagadambā, jagannādhaḥ, jadā, janakaḥ
jha-	jhadā, jhadiḥi, jhashaḥ
ñja-	añjali, añjanam, pañja
ṭa-	paṭaḥ, ṭaṅkaraḥ, ṭittibhaḥ
ṭha-	ṭhakkuraḥ, ṭheraḥ, pīṭhaḥ, paṭhati,
ḍa-	ḍamaru, ḍayanam, ḍāginí
ḍha-	ḍhakka, ḍholaḥ, ḍhalam
na-	veeṇa, praṇavam, prāṇaḥ

ta- taru, tāraḥ, tatvam, taṇdulaḥ

tha- rathā, kathā

da- daya, daridraḥ, divasaḥ, dantaḥ.

dha- dhanam, dhanyam, dhamaniḥi, dharmaḥ

na- nayanam, namaskāraḥ, nakṣatraḥ

pa- pañca, pakṣaḥ, paṅkajam, pañcamaḥ

pha- phalam, phaṇam, phalakam,

ba- bakulaḥ, balam, bahumānaḥ, balākaḥ

bha- bhaktaḥ, bhakṣaṇam, bhagavān, bhaṭaḥ

ma- madhu, matiḥi, madaḥ, madhurā

ya- yakṣaḥ, yajñaḥ, yajamānaḥ

ra- raktam, ragaḥ, ramaṇi, rātri

la- lakṣam, lakṣaṇam, lakṣmihi

va- vamśaḥ, varāḥ, vajraḥ, vatsalaḥ

śa- śakthiḥi, śareeram, śatam, śarkkara

ṣa - ṣad, ṣadaṅgam, ṣadānanam

sa- samskritaḥ, samskāraḥ, samrambhaḥ

ha- hamsaḥ, haraḥ, haritam, hariṇaḥ

kṣa- kṣaṇaḥ, kṣamā, kṣayaḥ, kṣīṇitaḥ

jña- prajña, jñanam, vijñanam

GLOSSARY

Advāsana: Adva – Prone; Āsana - Posture

Aṅgulīmūlaśakti : Strengthening Finger Joints

Aṅgulīśakti : Strengthening Finger Joints

Aṛdhacandrāsana: Ardha – Half; Candra – Moon; Crescent Moon Posture

Ardha Kapotāsana: Ardha – Half; Kapota - Pigeon

Ardhamatsyendrāsana: Ardha – Half; Matsyendra - Name of a sage;

Ardhapadmāsana: Ardha – Half; Padma – Lotus; Half Lotus Posture

Ardha Pavanamuktāsana: Ardha – Half; Pavana – Wind; Mukta – Relieving; Wind Relieving Posture

Ardha Śalabhāsana: Ardha – Half; Salabha - Locust

Ardha Pataṅgāsana : Half Butterfly

Ardha Uṣṭrāsana: Ardha – Half; Ustra – Camel; Camel Posture

Ardha Utkatāsana: Ardha - Half; Utkat - Squat Posture

Ardha Uttanāsana: Ardha – Half; Uttana - Intense Stretch Posture

Aśtānga Namaskārāsana – Aśtānga - eight arms; namaskār - prayer

Aśvasañchalanāsana: Equestrian Posture

Baddhakōnāsana: Baddha – Bound; Kona - Angle

Bālāsana: Bala – Child; Child Posture

Bhastrika: Bhastrika - Bellows

Bhrūmadhyadṛṣti: Eye gazing at centre of eyebrows

Bhujangāsana āsana: Bhujanga - Serpent

Bhūnamanāsana: Bhu – Earth; Naman - Prostrate/Salute/Posture

Bhrāmari: Bee

Catuṣpāda Pitham : Catus – Four; Pada – Legs; Pitham – Posture

Candra Bhedana : Chandra – Moon; Bhedana - Piercing

Daṇḍāsana: Danda – Stick; Āsana - Posture

Dhanurāsana: Dhanuhu- Bow; Bow Posture

Dṛṣticakra : Eye Rotation

Garudāsana: Garuda – Eagle; Āsana – Posture

Gomukhāsana : Go – Cow; Mukha – Face; Posture resembling a cow's face

Gūlpha Cakra : Ankle Rotation

Gūlpha Naman: Ankle Bending

Grīvaśakti : Neck Rotation

Halāsana: Hala - Plough

Hastagharṣaṇam : Palming
Hasta Uthānāsana: Hasta – Hand; Uttana – Upward Extension Posture
Drdhagati: Locomotive Walking Exercise
Drutagati: Locomotive running Exercise
Jalandharbandha : Jalandhra – Glottis; Bandha - Lock
Jaṅghaśaktivikāsa : Thigh and arm strengthening exercise
Janu Sirsāsana: Janu – Knee; Sirsa – Head; Head to knee posture
Kākacalanam : Crow Walk
Kākāsana: Crow Posture
Kapāla bhāti: Kapal – Skull; Bhati - Shining
Kapōlaśakti : Rejuvenating and strengthening eyes
Kara Prṣtha śakti: Wrist Bending
Karatalaśakti : Palms Bending
Karṇaśakti : Improving the power of hearing
Karnapidāsana: Karna – Ear; Pida - Pressure
Katicakrāsana: Kati – Waist; Cakra - Rotating Posture
Kūrparanamanam : Elbow Bending
Makarāsana: Makar - Crocodile
Maṇdukāsana: Manduka – Frog; Frog Posture
Maṇibandhaśakti : Wrist Rotation
Mārjārāsana: Marjari – Cat; Cat Posture
Matsyāsana: Matsya - Fish
Mrigi Mudrā: Mrigi – Deer; Mudrā - Symbol
Mūlabandha: Mula – Anus; Bandha – Lock
Nādi Sodana: Nadi – Channels; Sodana - Cleansing
Nāsikāgradṛṣti : Eye gazing at tip of the nose
Natrajāsana: Nataraja - Lord Of Dance; Āsana - Posture
Naukāsana: Nauka – Boat; Boat Posture
Netramardanam: Eye Pressing
Netraśakti : Eye Movements
Pādahastāsana: Pada – Feet; Hasta – Hand; Hand To Feet Posture
Pādāṅgulī Naman : Toe Bending
Padmāsana: Lotus Posture
Pārśvakōnāsana (Parivṛtta): Parivritti – Twist; Parsva – Lateral; Konāsana - Angled Posture
Pārśvakōnāsana Uthitha: Uthita – Standing; Parsva – Lateral; Konāsana - Angled Posture

Pārśva Uthānāsana: Parsva – Lateral; Uttana - Intense Stretch Posture

Parvatāsana: Parvat - Mountain Posture

Paśchimōthānāsana : Paschima – West; Intense stretch of the posterior

Pavanamuktāsana: Pavan – Wind; Mukta - Relieving

Pranamāsana: Pranam - Prayer Posture

Prasārita Pāda Uthānāsana: Prasarita – Spread; Pada - Legs

Pūrṇa Pataṅgāsana : Full Butterfly

Pūrvatanāsana: Purva – East; Uttana – Intense Stretch

Rekhāgati : Walking in a straight line

Śalabhāsana: Salabha - Locust

Samasthiti : Starting Position

Sarvaṅgāsana: Sarva – All; Anga – Limbs; Āsana - Posture

Sethubandhāsana: Setu – Bridge; Bandha – Bind; Bridge Posture

Ṣanmukhīmudrā : Shan – Six; Mukhi – Face; Mudrā - Symbol

Shashankāsana: Shash - Rabbit/hare; Ank – Lap; Rabbit Posture

Śavāsana: Shava – Corpse Posture

Śronī Cakra: Hip Socket Rotation

Sidhāsana: Siddha - Accomplished Posture

Simhāsana: Simha – Lion; Lion Posture

Śirṣāsana: Sirsa - Head

Śitalī: Cooling

Śītkari: Hissing

Skandharāsana : Skandha – Shoulder; Āsana - Posture

Skandacakra: Shoulder Rotation

Skandamūlaśakti: Shoulder Root Strengthening

Skanda Uttana śakti: Shoulder Stretch

Sukhāsana: Sukha - At Ease Posture

Supta Baddha Kōnāsana: Supta – Lying; Baddha – Bound; Kona - Angle

Supta Eka Padāṅguṣṭāsana: Supta – Lying; Ekapada - One Foot; Angustha - Big Toe

Supta Padāṅguṣṭāsana: Supta – Lying; Pada – Feet; Angustha – Big Toe

Supta Prasārita Padāṅguṣṭāsana: Supta – Lying; Prasarita – Spread; Pada – Feet; Angustha – Big Toe

Supta Vajrāsana: Supta – Lying; Vajrāsana – Diamond Posture

Sūrya Bhedana: Surya – Sun; Bhedana - Piercing

Tadāgīmudrā : Tadaka – Pond or Tank; Mudrā - Symbol

Tādāsana: Tada - Palm Tree; Āsana - Posture

Tiryak Bhujangāsana: Tiryaka – Twisting; Bhujanga - Cobra

Tiryak Tādāsana: Tiryaka - Swaying; Palm Tree Posture

Trikoṇāsana (Parivrtti): Twist

Trikoṇāsana (Parsva): Lateral; Trikona - Three Angle Posture

Udaraśakti : Strengthening Abdomen

Uddiyana Bandha: Uddiyana – Abdominal; Bandha - Lock

Ujjayi: Victorious

Upavista koṇāsana: Upavista – Seated; Kona - Angle

Urdhva Prasrita Padāsana: Urdhva – Upward; Prasrita – Extension; Pada - Leg

Uṣṭrāsana: Ustra – Camel; Camel Posture

Uthita Hasta Pādaṅguṣṭāsana: Uttita – Standing; Hasta – Hand; Padangustāsana - Raised hand to big toe posture

Utkatāsana: Utkat - Squat Posture

Uttan Maṇdukāsana: Uttan – Extend; Extended Frog Posture

Uttana Pristāsana: Uttan - Stretch Out; Pristha - Back of the body; Known as lizard posture

Uttanāsana: Intense Stretch Posture

Vajrāsana: Vajra - Diamond Posture

Vakrāsana: Vakra – Twist; Āsana - Posture

Vasisthāsana: Vasista – Name of a Sage; Rishi Posture

Viparītakarṇi : Viparita – Inversion; Karni - Doing

Vīrabhadrāsana: Vira-Brave; Bhadra - Warrior Posture

Vriksāsana: Tree Posture

Vyāghrāsana: Vyaghra – Tiger; Tiger Posture

Yogamudrāsana: Yoga – Union; Mudrā - Seal

REFERENCES

The following books have been referred to, while compiling this book:

- Patanjali Yoga Sutrā
- Hatha Yoga Pradīpika
- Gheranda Samhita
- Goraksha Samhita
- Shiva Samhita
- Hatha Ratnāvali

In addition, we have relied on the oral tradition of yogic knowledge for the details of a few practices such as Surya Namaskar and Light Yogic Exercises

Printed in Great Britain
by Amazon

87172211R00116